# The Evangelical
# Left

## Other Titles by Millard J. Erickson

# The Evangelical Left

*Encountering Postconservative Evangelical Theology*

## Millard J. Erickson

 BakerBooks

A Division of Baker Book House Co
Grand Rapids, Michigan 49516

Published by Baker Books
a division of Baker Book House Company
P.O. Box 6287, Grand Rapids, MI 49516–6287

Printed in the United States of America

**Library of Congress Cataloging-in-Publication Data**

Erickson, Millard J.
    The Evangelical Left : encountering postconservative Evangelical
theology / Millard J. Erickson.
       p.   cm.
    Includes bibliographical references and index.
    ISBN 0-8010-2140-5 (paper)
    1. Evangelicalism—North America—History—20th century.
  2. Theology, Doctrinal—North America—History—20th century.
  3. North America—Church history—20th century.
  4. Postconservatism.  I. Title.
  BR1642.N7E75   1997
  230'.04624—dc21                  97-1943

For information about academic books, resources for Christian leaders,
and all new releases available from Baker Book House, visit our web site:
http://www.bakerbooks.com

To my brother
Robert O. Erickson

# Contents

# Preface

**To** any astute observer of the contemporary American religious scene, it is apparent that some interesting theological developments are occurring within evangelicalism. For some of the commonplace doctrinal distinctives of the previous generation of evangelicalism are being redefined. It is to examine this trend, which recently has taken on an identity as postconservative evangelicalism, that this book is written.

This is not intended to be an alarmist book, warning against heresies. It is, however, intended to be an "alertist" book, calling Christians to take careful note of theological developments and weigh their soundness. As John wrote his readers to "test the spirits" (1 John 4:1), so this is a call to scrutiny and evaluation. Because the movement is still taking shape, this brief book is only an introduction to what we may expect to see in the years to come.

The ideas in this book have been tested publicly in a number of settings. Parts of it were used in a Doctor of Ministry seminar at Grace Theological Seminary, Winona Lake, Indiana, June 19–20, 1995; in a faculty seminar during Scholars in Ministry Week at Southwestern Baptist Theological Seminary, Fort Worth, Texas, February 8, 1996; and as the Issachar Lectures at Grace Covenant Church, Austin, Texas, April, 26–27, 1996. The entire manuscript was presented as lectures in a course at Associated Canadian Theological Schools, Langley, British Columbia, July 22–26, 1996. Interaction with numerous persons present on those occasions have helped sharpen my thinking. Maria denBoer has enhanced the manuscript with her accurate and gracious editing.

# 1 Postconservative Evangelical Theology in Context

**To** set the stage for our consideration of the importance of theology, I would first like to consider a somewhat different topic, drawn from the realm of health. A few years ago, an experiment was conducted involving two groups. These groups were made up of comparable subjects, five in the first group and four in the second. Their occupations, activities, and backgrounds were similar, but there was one significant difference in their diets. Over a sixteen-year period, the two groups were tested in terms of their ability to perform one particular act of physical strength. The results are portrayed in the two charts below. In the case of each

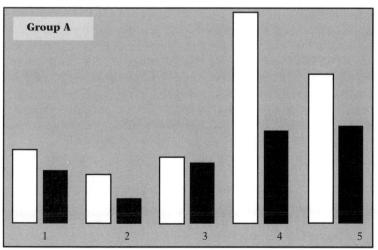

Group A

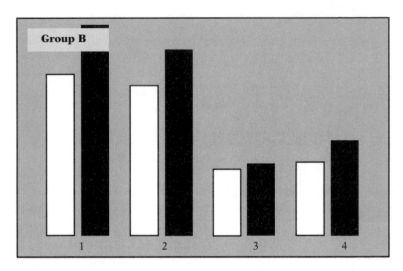

subject, the light bar represents the results of the test in 1972; the dark bar, the results of the same test administered in 1988.

For group A, whatever variable was involved, it is apparent that it was not a positive influence. Although the amount of decline varies with each subject, in each case, there is a definite loss of strength. Now let us see what the effects were on the other group. Although drawn to a different scale than the first chart, the relationships among the individuals in each group are accurate.

It is apparent that the results were quite different for the two groups. The members of group A declined considerably—in some cases, quite dramatically—in their ability to perform this piece of work. Group B, on the other hand, showed increased ability in this particular function. Although the test groups were small, they showed such significant differences we must conclude that the one differing factor was a powerful one indeed.

What was this difference in diet? Certainly physicians, dietitians, and public health officials would want to know, so that they can recommend its use.

And now I have a confession to make. What you have just read is actually a parable. We are not talking about medical patients, diets, or physical strength. The two groups are actually two groups of Christian foreign mission organizations. Group A consists of several denominations that are commonly referred to as "mainline." These are old, quite large denominations. With some exceptions in each group, they are relatively liberal in theology. Group B consists of one large denominational group, a nondenominational mission board, and a number of independent and denominational mission boards affiliated with two associations of mission boards. They are all conservative or evangelical in their theology. The single major difference between the first group and the second group is theological. The test scores referred to are not measures of physical strength and ability to perform work, but number of foreign missionaries under appointment. As can be seen from the graphs, groups that are liberal in theology had a marked decline in the number of missionaries serving under their board, while the theologically conservative Christian organizations increased significantly the number of missionaries supported over the sixteen-year period. When interpreted, the parable reads as follows.[1]

| Group A | 1972 | 1988 |
| --- | --- | --- |
| 1. American Baptist Churches | 262 | 179 |
| 2. Episcopal Church | 165 | 72 |
| 3. United Church of Christ | 244 | 214 |
| 4. United Methodist Church | 951 | 416 |
| 5. United Presbyterian Church, U.S.A. | 604 | 435 |

| Group B | | |
| --- | --- | --- |
| 1. Evangelical Foreign Missions Association | 7,074 | 9,000+ |
| 2. Interdenominational Foreign Missions Association | 6,130 | 8,000+ |
| 3. Wycliffe Bible Translators | 2,200 | 2,269 |
| 4. Southern Baptist Convention | 2,507 | 3,839 |

1. *Missions Handbook: North American Protestant Ministries Overseas*, 10th ed. (Monrovia, Calif.: MARC, 1973), pp. 115, 345, 361, 374, 378, 407, 424, 382, 426; *Missions Handbook: USA/Canada Protestant Ministries Overseas*, 14th ed., ed. W. Dayton Roberts and John A. Siewert (Monrovia, Calif.: MARC, 1989), pp. 73, 82, 131, 211, 223, 231, 232, 247. The 14th edition is the last edition for which statistics are comparable to those of earlier editions, since later editions reflect an increasing percentage of short-term missionaries.

The same pattern of decline and growth revealed in the landmark article, "The Missionary Retreat," fifteen years earlier has continued, with the growth of the evangelical missions being less dramatic than before.[2]

The statistics could be repeated for other measures, such as number of church members and attendees; financial giving, especially as a percentage of income; and related matters. Indeed, these disparities between more liberal groups and more conservative groups were sufficient to lead Dean Kelley, a United Methodist minister and official of the National Council of Churches, to write a book entitled *Why Conservative Churches Are Growing.*[3]

Statistics are not infallible measures of religious vitality and integrity, and we need to beware of measuring success, effectiveness, or faithfulness to the Lord of the church using purely pragmatic factors. Growth of any organism can be the result of many factors, some of them unhealthy. As a doctor friend of mine once pointed out, the most rapidly growing human body cells are malignant cells. But the statistics should cause us to stop and ponder carefully the importance of theology, especially when we are considering such a crucial factor as obedience to the Great Commission that Jesus gave to his disciples and to the entire church.

The theologians and other leaders who led those denominations down the path that they did thought they were doing a positive service to the church and to Jesus. Yet decades later the fruits of those efforts are apparent in the lack of vitality of groups that adopted them. It is important that evangelicals ask whether they now stand where some of these other Christian groups did earlier in the century, and what can be done to ensure that the story is not repeated. George Santayana's famous statement that those who fail to learn from the past are condemned to repeat it is very pertinent here.

To detect this change or shift is not as easy as we might think, however. For a study of twentieth-century church his-

2. "The Missionary Retreat," *Christianity Today* 16.4 (November 19, 1971): 26, 27. For comparability, the same missions that were the subject of that article have also been used in our study.

3. Dean Kelley, *Why Conservative Churches Are Growing* (New York: Harper and Row, 1972).

tory will reveal that the change is not always signaled or identified by those who are making it. Indeed, some who considered themselves liberals or modernizers continued to use the same terminology, but invested it with different meaning. This meant that some traditional believers thought that the old meaning was still held and taught, but meanwhile a new meaning or content was being taught to those who had not been previously exposed to the concepts and terms. This brought an interesting comment from an unexpected source: "In these contentions the Fundamentalists are correct: it is precisely the abandonment of such doctrines which the Modernists desire to effect in the Protestant churches; and to an impartial observer there does seem in the liberal positions much confusion and lack of precise thinking, as well as the appearance at least of a lack of frankness and a fondness for esoteric 'reinterpretation' that may approach in its effects actual hypocrisy."[4] John Herman Randall Jr., at the time professor of philosophy at Columbia University, was certainly not a fundamentalist sympathizer, being at most a humanist religiously.

Another example of redefinition can be found within the Roman Catholic Church. The traditional position on the extent of salvation was expressed in the formula, "outside the Church, no salvation." One could be saved or rendered just in God's sight only by being a full communicant member of the Roman Catholic Church and receiving grace through its sacraments. The formula is still used as an expression of the Church's position. Yet the actual content of the formula's meaning has been altered through a redefinition of the expression "outside the Church." The Second Vatican Council declared that there are three degrees of membership in the Church. Roman Catholics in good standing are "fully incorporated into" the Church. Other, non-Catholic Christians are "linked to" the Church. Those of other religions than Christianity, even nonreligious persons of good will, are "related to" the Church.[5] Thus, while

4. John Herman Randall Jr., *The Making of the Modern Mind: A Survey of the Intellectual Background of the Present Age*, rev. ed. (Boston: Houghton Mifflin, 1940), p. 542.

5. *The Documents of Vatican II*, ed. Walter M. Abbott (New York: Guild Press, 1966), vol. 13, pp. 32–34.

retaining the original terms, the meaning of the formula has been changed considerably.

In light of these examples, it is important that evangelicals ask not only for the formulas of belief but for the actual content of those formulas or expressions. Sometimes lay persons are so conditioned to respond to particular expressions to which an emotional conditioning has been attached that they fail to determine the real meaning. In a day in which meaning is thought by some to reside, not objectively in the words and expressions themselves, but in the person who receives them so that its meaning is what it means to the recipient, this concern is especially appropriate.

## The History of Evangelicalism

Evangelicalism is a branch of Christianity which, as its name would suggest, places a strong emphasis on the gospel, or the εὐαγγέλιον. As such, most evangelicals would maintain that they trace their heritage back to the New Testament itself. They would contend that the movement that dates from approximately the eighteenth century is not an innovation, but actually represents a return to the original teaching and experience that Jesus himself introduced. Although sometimes held and practiced by only a minority of persons within the broad church, it has always been present.

It was, however, in the eighteenth century that this movement took on a special identity. A number of events can be seen as formative. One was the conversion of John Wesley. Raised in the Anglican Church and having served as a missionary to the colony of Georgia, he sensed a lack in his own life. He said, "I who went to America to convert the Indians was never myself converted."[6] On the evening of May 24, 1738, he attended a meeting of a Moravian Brethren group on Aldersgate Street in London. He heard the reading of Luther's preface to the Epistle to the Romans, and, as he put it, his heart was "strangely warmed."[7] From that experience came the great Wesleyan revival and the Methodist Church.

6. John Wesley, *The Heart of John Wesley's Journal* (New Canaan, Conn.: Keats, 1979), entry of Sunday, January 28, 1738, p. 31.
7. Ibid., entry of Wednesday, May 24, 1738, p. 43.

In the American colonies, the Great Awakenings were the basis of a major evangelical surge. The First Great Awakening was actually a series of religious revivals, beginning about 1725 and continuing until about 1760. Jonathan Edwards was a major force in this movement, but probably the one person who played the largest role in linking these various occurrences into the awakening was George Whitefield, a colleague of John Wesley. Coming to the colonies in 1740, he traveled widely as an itinerant evangelist. The awakening was characterized by a strong emphasis on personal repentance of sin and conversion, but also by a strong concern for social justice and education. Early opposition to the practice of slavery was fostered by the revivals, and a number of institutions of higher education, including Princeton, Brown, and Dartmouth, were founded.[8] The Second Great Awakening, from about 1795 to 1830, was more theologically diffuse, involving the more Arminian views of Nathaniel Taylor and Charles Finney. The First Awakening had been largely Calvinistic and more theologically oriented. Out of this Second Awakening also grew the later revivalism of the American frontier.[9]

This concern for personal conversion as well as for combatting social evil also characterized evangelicalism in the nineteenth century. In many cases, evangelicals were at the forefront of efforts to combat evils in society.[10] This was true with respect to the abolitionist and prohibitionist movements. In the latter half of the nineteenth century, however, there developed within many Protestant denominations the movement known as theological liberalism or modernism. This represented the impact on theology and church life of some of the modern learning, such as evolution and literary-historical criticism. The liberals believed that these developments must be accepted and theological understanding adapted to them.

For many Christians in established denominations, these developments were disconcerting. It appeared to them that their

8. Edwin Scott Gaustad, *The Great Awakening in New England* (New York: Harper and Brothers, 1957).

9. Charles Roy Keller, *The Second Great Awakening in Connecticut* (Hamden, Conn.: Archon, 1968).

10. Timothy Smith, *Revivalism and Social Reform in Mid-Nineteenth-Century America* (Abingdon, 1957); Norris Magnuson, *Salvation in the Slums: Evangelical Social Work, 1865–1920* (Grand Rapids: Baker, 1990).

fellow Baptists, Presbyterians, and Congregationalists were abandoning the very essence of the Christian faith in their attempt to be modern. They found that in many cases they had more in common with conservative Christians from other traditions than with these Christians within their own denominations. Some of them used to attend Bible conferences, summer gatherings that combined biblical preaching and teaching with recreation. At one of these, the Niagara Conference in 1895, a list of basic beliefs was drawn up, which those attending considered to embody the core of what it meant to be a Christian in terms of doctrinal teachings. These beliefs were thought to be the irreducible basis of Christian fellowship. This process of articulating the essential Christian doctrines was repeated in other circles, and in time they were called the "fundamentals" of the Christian faith. They included such basics as belief in the bodily resurrection and substitutionary atonement of Jesus Christ. The term "fundamentalist" was probably coined by Curtis Lee Laws, editor of the Baptist *Watchman-Examiner*, about 1910, to identify a person who insisted on the indispensability of these very basic doctrines. This word quickly caught on and a grassroots movement was transformed into virtually a political party within denominations and a segment of society in general.

In the first decade of the century, fundamentalism was simply an attempt to give a defense of what had traditionally been Christianity. This was done, first, through offering scholarly expositions and defenses of these foundational doctrines. Although the lists of fundamentals varied, they usually included such items as the inerrancy of the Bible; the historicity of biblical miracles, especially those of Jesus Christ; the virgin birth of Christ; the bodily resurrection of Christ; and the substitutionary atonement. This exposition and defense was especially carried out through the preparation and circulation of a series of booklets, each dealing with a different doctrine, entitled *The Fundamentals*. Their publication and distribution were financed by two wealthy California laymen, Lyman and Milton Stewart.[11] The authors of the articles were competent, careful scholars, representing a number of denominational connec-

11. *The Fundamentals: A Testimony to the Truth*, ed. George M. Marsden (New York: Garland, 1988).

tions; the booklets covered the specific points of interpretation of such doctrines as creation and the nature of biblical inspiration. Such luminaries as James Orr, B. B. Warfield, John C. Ryle, and H. C. G. Moule were authors of the pamphlets.

Gradually the nature of fundamentalism began to change. As liberalism became more vocal and influential in the various denominations, emphasis switched from affirmation of and argumentation for fundamental doctrines to criticism and rebuttal of the teachings of more liberal theologians. Fundamentalists sought to distinguish their own views from those of the liberals. Liberals were substituting a "social gospel" that attempted to transform the structures of society for the traditional gospel of personal regeneration through faith in Christ and acceptance of his atoning work. Liberals believed that individuals sinned at least in part because of the influence of a corrupt society. In their judgment, evil could only be combatted by altering these social situations.[12] To fundamentalists, however, modernists seemed to be treating the symptoms rather than the central problem. They wanted to make clear that they did not hold to the social gospel and all that was involved in that view. So they emphasized more and more the dimension of personal regeneration, and neglected the social application of the gospel, which had so strongly characterized the evangelicalism of the nineteenth century and earlier. A narrowing of the classical evangelical position was the result.[13]

Gradually fundamentalism also shifted its strategy from scholarly argumentation to political effort, both within the church and within society in general. So, in the latter case, since evolution was perceived to be one of the most threatening elements of the modern learning, fundamentalists were instrumental in having a number of state legislatures, particularly in Southern states, pass laws forbidding its teaching in public schools. One of these laws, in Tennessee, led to the famous Scopes trial—or, as it was sometimes derisively referred to, the "monkey trial." John Scopes, a high school biology teacher in

12. Walter Rauschenbusch, *A Theology for the Social Gospel* (New York: Macmillan, 1917).

13. Carl F. H. Henry, *The Uneasy Conscience of Modern Fundamentalism* (Grand Rapids: Eerdmans, 1947), pp. 16–23.

Dayton, Tennessee, was brought to trial on the charge of having taught evolution in violation of state law. Two nationally known attorneys, Clarence Darrow and William Jennings Bryan, entered the case as members of the defense and prosecuting attorneys' teams, respectively. Bryan had been three times the unsuccessful Democratic nominee for president; Darrow was a widely known defense attorney and agnostic. Thus, what would ordinarily have been an obscure case in a small town became a matter of national, even international, attention. The question of Scopes' guilt was quickly and easily established. Then, however, Darrow was able to put Bryan on the witness stand. In his questioning, he succeeded in showing that Bryan, the outspoken defender of creation and critic of evolution, really did not have very extensive knowledge of biological science. Bryan, for example, had criticized the evolutionists' argument from similarities by noting that there is milk in a coconut, a milkweed, and a cow, but that no one contends that one is biologically derived from another.[14] The press covering the trial portrayed Bryan as a narrow-minded ignoramus, and the image was transferred to fundamentalists as a whole. They were depicted as opponents of academic freedom who were attempting by legal means to force their views on the public. Many of the anti-evolution laws remained upon the books of the states although they were no longer enforced.

The other strategy employed by fundamentalists was to oppose liberalism in the denominations. This was done by seeking to prevent the teaching of liberal views in seminaries and appointing liberal persons as foreign missionaries. They endeavored to elect to positions of control within the denominations persons who held the fundamental beliefs. Gradually, however, their strength waned as that of liberals increased. This can be seen most clearly in the Presbyterian denomination, for theology was of real importance to Presbyterians. Each year the liberals and the fundamentalists would nominate a candidate for moderator of the denomination. At first, the fundamentalist candidate would win; however, the margin of the vote declined year by year. Finally, in 1926, the fundamentalists were unsuccessful in electing their candidate—an

14. "Notes and Comments," *The Bible Champion* 30.4 (April 1924): 200.

indication that the balance of strength had swung to the liberal side.[15]

Other signs of the fundamentalists' decline were also evident in their failure to control the church's institutions. In the 1890s, the Presbyterian Church complained to one of its seminaries, Union Seminary in New York City, about the teaching of an Old Testament professor, Charles Briggs, and ordered the seminary to dismiss him. Instead, the seminary chose to retain Briggs and sever its ties with the Presbyterian Church.[16] By the late 1920s, the situation was reversed. The struggle was most clearly seen at the premier Presbyterian seminary, Princeton. Once a bastion of orthodoxy with the teaching of B. B. Warfield, Charles Hodge, and others, the Princeton faculty now was composed of individuals holding a mixture of viewpoints. The best known of the conservative faculty was J. Gresham Machen, whose New Testament scholarship had received widespread recognition. Over the years he had gradually shifted his interest and writing to apologetic issues, such as the virgin birth and the origin of Paul's religion, in books bearing those titles. Consequently, he was nominated for the chair of apologetics at the seminary. Rather than approving the nomination, however, the delegates to the General Assembly of the Church deferred action, instead appointing a committee to investigate the situation at Princeton Seminary. This led to the creation of two boards to control the school, leaving the important matters of governance to a new, more liberal board. Seeing the handwriting on the wall, Machen, together with O. T. Allis, Robert Dick Wilson, and others, withdrew and formed a new school, Westminster Seminary in Philadelphia, to carry on the tradition of orthodox scholarship. When they created a new foreign mission board, they were expelled from the Presbyterian Church, U.S.A., and subsequently founded a new denomination, the Orthodox Presbyterian Church.[17]

This pattern of the fundamentalists' defeat and withdrawal was repeated in several other denominations, as well as within

15. Norman F. Furniss, *The Fundamentalist Controversy, 1918–1931* (New Haven: Yale University Press, 1954), p. 137.

16. Steward G. Cole, *The History of Fundamentalism* (New York: Richard R. Smith, 1931), p. 122.

17. Ned B. Stonehouse, *J. Gresham Machen* (Grand Rapids: Eerdmans, 1954), pp. 389–90, 418, 459, 482.

the broader society. One would have expected that the movement would simply fade away. To the surprise of many observers, however, fundamentalism grew in strength. Now that the conservatives were separated from the more liberal churches, the statistics of both types of Christian churches could be more accurately assessed and compared. In terms of several objective measures, fundamentalists were outstripping liberals: church membership, volunteers for the ministry, and per capita giving.[18] The latter item was particularly surprising, since in many cases, fundamentalist churches drew their members from lower socioeconomic classes than did liberals. And, although they had lost their major academic institutions, they were establishing new schools, such as Westminster Theological Seminary and Dallas Theological Seminary.

Beyond this, however, a new movement soon emerged within evangelicalism. A handful of leaders began to speak critically of the shortcomings of fundamentalism and to call for a renewal of sorts. One of these was Harold John Ockenga, pastor of the historic Park Street Church in Boston. He published an article, "Can Fundamentalism Win America?" in *Christian Life and Times*, in which he answered the question essentially by saying, "not as presently constituted."[19]

Another individual who shared this concern for reforming fundamentalism was Carl F. H. Henry, a young theology professor at Northern Baptist Theological Seminary in Chicago. In *The Uneasy Conscience of Modern Fundamentalism*,[20] he challenged fundamentalism's abandonment of emphasis on the social dimensions of the gospel. In *Remaking the Modern Mind*,[21] he rejected the approach of Enlightenment thinking that left no room for the supernatural. It was an example of the type of scholarship that he called for fundamentalism to produce.

18. William Hordern, *New Directions in Theology Today:* vol. 1, *Introduction* (Philadelphia: Westminster, 1966), pp. 75–76.
19. Harold Ockenga, "Can Fundamentalism Win America?" *Christian Life and Times* 2.6 (June 1947): 13–15.
20. Carl F. H. Henry, *The Uneasy Conscience of Modern Fundamentalism* (Grand Rapids: Eerdmans, 1947).
21. Carl F. H. Henry, *Remaking the Modern Mind* (Grand Rapids: Eerdmans, 1948).

This new movement soon took on a name. Henry had written of a new evangelicalism, a term popularized by Harold John Ockenga in a convocation address.[22] This emphasis, or collection of emphases, called for evangelicalism to return to the heritage it had before and during the early days of the fundamentalist movement. This included careful, competent, scholarly defense of the Christian faith, emphasis on its social application, and avoidance of an extreme separatism that withdrew from fellowship with those who were not doctrinally pure.

The movement also began to take on institutional structure. In 1942, Ockenga and others organized the National Association of Evangelicals. It was intended to be an alternative to the liberal National Council of Churches, but without the negativism of the American Council of Churches, which Carl McIntire had pioneered. Then, in 1947, Fuller Theological Seminary was founded in Pasadena, California. The special project of radio evangelist Charles H. Fuller, it was intended to carry on his evangelistic and evangelical emphasis, combined with the very best of biblical and theological scholarship. It was designed to be a West Coast version of what Princeton Theological Seminary had been in the late nineteenth century. Ockenga was the first president, commuting initially from Boston with the intention that he would soon relocate to California. Henry was one of the four original faculty members.

A faculty member added in the second year of the school's existence exemplified both the genius and the dilemma of the school. Edward John Carnell already possessed the Doctor of Theology degree from Harvard Divinity School and was a candidate for the Doctor of Philosophy degree from Boston University. He had authored an apologetics textbook that had won the Eerdmans Publishing Company's $5,000 first prize for text-

---

22. The first public use of the label "new evangelical," in 1948, is widely attributed to Ockenga and even claimed by him, in the foreword to Harold Lindsell, *The Battle for the Bible* (Grand Rapids: Zondervan, 1976), p. 11. Henry, however, had used the term in three articles earlier that year in *Christian Life and Times:* "The Vigor of the New Evangelicalism," 3.1 (January 1948): 30–32; 3.3 (March 1948): 35–38, 85; 3.4 (April 1948): 32–35, 65–69. Cf. George M. Marsden, *Reforming Fundamentalism: Fuller Seminary and the New Evangelicalism* (Grand Rapids: Eerdmans, 1987), p. 146.

books. The son of a fundamentalist Baptist pastor, he wanted to go beyond the strictures of fundamentalism to present a rational defense of classical orthodoxy.[23]

Other facets of the movement began to emerge. A young evangelist, Billy Graham, had become Youth for Christ's first evangelist. After serving for a short time as president of Northwestern Schools in Minneapolis, he began the Billy Graham Evangelistic Association. His crusades began to attract large numbers of people. He reiterated the common fundamentalist message of the necessity of personal conversion and new birth, but conducted his crusades in a way that no fundamentalist would. He insisted that every effort be made to enlist the cooperation and participation of all the churches in the area where the crusade was being held, including those more liberal in theology as well as traditional fundamentalists. His messages gradually began to show a less rigidly literal approach to the Bible, and he increasingly began to speak out against social evils.[24]

Another major institutional step was taken in 1956. A new periodical, *Christianity Today*, was launched. Conceived of as a rival to the *Christian Century*, it quickly outstripped the latter in subscriptions. Henry, who in his earlier years had been a newspaper writer, was appointed editor, an indication of the nature and purpose of the publication. It was intended to be an articulate voice of evangelical theology, delivered at a level accessible to the average pastor. While it was especially a positive affirmation and argumentation for conservative doctrine, the articles did not hesitate to point out the shortcomings of more liberal theology, and Henry's editorials frequently seized on especially timely doctrinal issues as well as topics in social ethics.[25]

It appeared that all was well with the movement. A striking reversal of fortunes had taken place within conservative Protestantism. Steps had been successfully taken to combat the

23. Rudolf Nelson, *The Making and Unmaking of an Evangelical Mind: The Case of Edward Carnell* (Cambridge: Cambridge University Press, 1987), pp. 54–57.

24. Stanley High, *Billy Graham* (New York: McGraw-Hill, 1956), pp. 62–64.

25. Carl F. H. Henry, "Why 'Christianity Today'?" *Christianity Today* 1.1 (October 15, 1956): 20–21.

weaknesses that were all too evident within fundamentalism. The social dimension of the gospel was being addressed. Theological scholarship was flourishing. Not only at Fuller, but at numerous other institutions, faculty possessing doctorates from some of the finest graduate schools in the United States and abroad were teaching and writing, and their productions were being taken seriously. A professional society, the Evangelical Theological Society, had been founded in 1949, and its members were preparing and delivering scholarly papers. The heritage of fundamentalism in its worst dimensions seemed to have been left behind.

It soon became apparent that not all was well, however. Cracks began to appear in the New Evangelicalism, not on the right, but on the left. The leaders of the movement had believed that they had positioned themselves the ideal distance from fundamentalism, but some of the newer additions did not stop at that point. By 1954, it had become apparent both that Ockenga would not leave his Boston pulpit to become full-time resident president of Fuller and that the institution could not continue with the sort of part-time arrangement that had been in place for six years. In the end, the search process focused on someone within the faculty: Carnell. He came to the position with the idea of being a scholar-president. He also sounded, in his inauguration address, a call for the seminary to exercise tolerance toward those who did not share its doctrinal convictions.[26] In some of his writings during this period, Carnell sought to distance himself from many of the fundamentalist attitudes and practices.[27] Although to the end of his life he maintained a conservative theological position, Carnell during his five-year presidency encouraged trends that would go well beyond his original intention.

The first strong indication of a real divergence within the camp of the New Evangelicalism appeared on what has come to be known as "Black Saturday," December 1, 1962. The Fuller faculty were holding their ten-year planning retreat, and Daniel Fuller, son of the founder, just returned from studying in Swit-

26. Marsden, *Reforming Fundamentalism*, pp. 141–52.
27. E.g., *The Case for Orthodox Theology* (Philadelphia: Westminster, 1959), pp. 113–26.

zerland, was the dean-elect of the school. Urged by one of the school's administrators to speak out forcefully on matters if he was to establish his leadership, Fuller chose to address the issue of biblical inerrancy. He contended there were errors in the Bible that could not be accounted for as copyists' errors. He suggested instead that the Bible was fully truthful and free from all error when referring to revelational or doctrinal matters, matters pertaining to salvation, but that it was not inerrant in matters of science and history. Others who had earlier expressed some reservations about inerrancy, such as William LaSor and George Ladd, sided with Fuller on this matter, whereas Carnell spoke strongly in opposition. While the faculty had continued to sign annually "without mental reservation" a statement that the Bible was "free from all error, in the whole and in the part," it was now apparent that there was no real unanimity on this matter.[28] The selection of David Hubbard as the school's new president, taking office in 1963, began a stronger trend to the left. Henry had left in 1956 to take the *Christianity Today* post. The departure of Harold Lindsell to *Christianity Today* and of Wilbur Smith and Gleason Archer to Trinity Evangelical Divinity School, together with the death of Carnell in 1967, depleted the school of its most vocal conservative spokespersons.[29] Their positions were filled with less orthodox individuals.

Other signs began to appear, indicating a continued leftward movement of some evangelicals. In 1974, Richard Quebedeaux published a book entitled *The Young Evangelicals*, in which he expressed appreciation and admiration for the evangelical left.[30] In 1978 he published another book, *The Worldly Evangelicals*. Here he notes the continued theological shift of this group. His assessment in the preface is an interesting study: "I am not quite as optimistic and uncritical in treating the evangelical left as I was five years ago. At that time I assumed that evangelicals could be genuinely faithful to the Gospel (and 'progressive') only insofar as they became more like—but not

28. Marsden, *Reforming Fundamentalism*, pp. 208–15.

29. Ibid., pp. 215–24.

30. Richard Quebedeaux, *The Young Evangelicals* (San Francisco: Harper and Row, 1974).

too much like—liberals. However, now that this liberalizing tendency among evangelicals is readily apparent and growing, I'm no longer certain that it is a good thing at all."[31] Much of the material in the book is anecdotal, but significant. Quebedeaux notes shifts both in doctrine and in lifestyle. He suggests that the behavior of these evangelicals is considerably less different from that of liberal Christians and of non-Christians than had formerly been the case with evangelicals. Near the end of the book he writes:

> In the past disgruntled evangelicals readily became liberal in word and deed. . . . Now, however, the evangelical left provides a better option for evangelicals who may still *believe* like evangelicals, but wish to *behave* like liberals. Furthermore, among this group there may be an increasingly large number of people who really *have* moved beyond evangelical belief toward liberalism. . . . Thus some evangelicals *are* becoming liberals without saying so. But it is still too early to discern where this current trend will lead.[32]

What Quebedeaux had reported in anecdotal and often undocumented fashion, James Davison Hunter documented with research a decade later. Hunter, a sociologist at the University of Virginia, surveyed faculty and students at nine evangelical liberal arts colleges and seven evangelical seminaries. What he found was both interesting, and to many evangelicals, alarming. Because his book dealt with the views of evangelical students and those who teach them, it gave a good indication of where evangelicalism was likely to go in the years ahead. It showed a considerably increased openness on the part of these young evangelicals to views previously associated with more liberal movements: "For what one finds is a brand of theology that for generations had been considered 'modernistic' being advocated by theologians who vigorously defend their right to use the name of evangelical."[33] This departure from the ortho-

31. Richard Quebedeaux, *The Worldly Evangelicals* (San Francisco: Harper and Row, 1978), p. xii.

32. Ibid., pp. 166–67.

33. James Davison Hunter, *Evangelicalism: The Coming Generation* (Chicago: University of Chicago Press, 1987), p. 32.

dox or conservative view is especially notable among the college faculty surveyed, particularly those teaching in the humanities and social sciences. As Hunter puts it, "There is, among many faculty, a sense that true and vital Christianity depends upon a debunking of many of the traditions of conservative Protestantism. Their task, in part, is one of liberation."[34]

There were also indications in Hunter's study that the changes taking place were occurring rather silently and covertly. He says, "It is difficult to assess just how far these trends have gone or for how many these developments represent the cutting edge for Evangelical theology. The issues are highly sensitive in Evangelical circles and those who hold such positions would not be likely to advertise what they know others consider to be suspect if not heretical."[35] Earlier, an outside but sympathetic observer of evangelical theology, William Hordern, had called attention to the presence within evangelicalism of a tendency similar to that described above in connection with liberalism and Roman Catholicism. This is the practice of retaining a theological term and changing its content. Writing of what he terms the "new conservatives," he says, "To both the fundamentalist and the nonconservative, it often seems that the new conservative is trying to say, 'The Bible is inerrant, but of course this does not mean it is without errors.'"[36]

It is quite possible, then, that the movement now coming to be known as "postconservative evangelicalism" is not something really new. It is simply a movement that has been developing for some time, but now has become visible as its advocates begin to speak more plainly. We need now to describe some of its general motifs and identify some of its advocates before going on to a more complete examination of these issues.

Roger Olson, in a May 1995 article in *Christian Century*, sought to give some definition to this movement. He observed that in the minds of most persons, both within and outside

34. Ibid., p. 176.
35. Ibid., p. 33.
36. William Hordern, *New Directions in Theology Today*, vol. 1, *Introduction* (Philadelphia: Westminster, 1966), p. 83.

evangelicalism, "evangelical" and "theologically conservative" are synonymous, but that some who identify themselves as evangelical are "shedding theological conservatism."[37] He noted several characteristics of this theology:[38]

1. Eagerness to engage in dialogue with nonevangelical theologians. Indeed, "they seek opportunities to converse with those whom conservative evangelicals would probably consider enemies."
2. Concern with theology's domination by white males and Eurocentrism. Recognizing the influence of social location on theological work, postconservatives seek to include women, persons of color, and Third World Christians in theological scholarship.
3. Broadening of the sources used in theology. This frequently includes an emphasis on "narrative-shaped experience" rather than "propositional truths enshrined in doctrines." The sources may include, in addition to the Bible, Christian tradition, culture, and contemporary Christian experience.
4. A discontent with the traditional ties of evangelical theology to the "evangelical Enlightenment," especially commonsense realism.
5. Rejection of the "wooden" approach to Scripture, in favor of regarding it as "Spirit-inspired realistic narrative."
6. An open view of God, in which God limits himself and enters into relationships of genuine response to humans, taking their pain and suffering into himself. God is a risk-taker, not one who controls everything so that nothing contrary to his desires can occur.
7. An acceptance, rather than a rejection, of the realm of nature. Nature, although fallen, is never abandoned by grace, which then pervades it.

37. Roger E. Olson, "Postconservative Evangelicals Greet the Postmodern Age," *Christian Century* 112.15 (May 3, 1995): 480.

38. A similar list appears in Clark H. Pinnock, *Tracking the Maze: Finding Our Way Through Modern Theology from an Evangelical Perspective* (San Francisco: Harper and Row, 1990), pp. 67–68. Pinnock raises the question of whether these changes will lead to a new wave of liberal theology, and answers it in the negative (pp. 68–69).

8. A hope for a near-universal salvation. God has not left himself without a witness in all cultures, sufficient to bring people to salvation if they earnestly seek it.
9. An emphasis in Christology on the humanity of Jesus. While retaining belief in the divinity of Christ, this is thought of more in relational than in substance and person categories.
10. A more synergistic understanding of salvation. These theologians are, overall, more Arminian than Calvinistic.
11. A rejection of triumphalism with respect to theological truth-claims. Postconservatives are critical of belief in epistemological certainty and theological systems.

Who are these postconservative evangelicals, and where are they to be found? Certainly the most prominent institution of this movement is Fuller Theological Seminary. Some had been surprised at Quebedeaux's speculation that Fuller Seminary might eventually become "the leading center of neo-orthodox conviction in the world—both in theology and in the critical study of Scripture."[39] Time and events, however, have shown him insightful. Hunter's research documented what many have long known: that many traditionally evangelical liberal arts college faculty members have moved well beyond the usual bounds of conservative theology. This is especially true of professors in the humanities and the social sciences.[40] InterVarsity Press publishes a large number of the books written in this strain of evangelicalism. Even the venerable *Christianity Today*, founded as a bulwark of conservative theology, has broadened its orientation to more practical and popular topics, and has become more of a Christian newsmagazine, as David Wells has documented through content analysis of its articles.[41]

In terms of individuals, probably the best known theologian who has produced the most published material and over the longest period of time is Clark Pinnock, professor of theology

39. Quebedeaux, *Worldly Evangelicals*, p. 100.
40. Hunter, *Evangelicalism*, pp. 173–76.
41. David Wells, *No Place for Truth or Whatever Happened to Evangelical Theology?* (Grand Rapids: Eerdmans, 1993), pp. 207–11.

at McMaster Divinity College in Hamilton, Ontario. His work ranges over many of the topics of theology. John Sanders, instructor in theology at Oak Hills Bible College, Bemidji, Minnesota, has been closely allied with Pinnock in the areas of salvation and the doctrine of God. Stanley Grenz, professor of theology at Carey Theological College, Vancouver, British Columbia, outlined his agenda for the restructuring of evangelical theology in his *Revisioning Evangelical Theology.* His *Theology for the People of God* is the first complete systematic theology to appear from this group. Numerous other less well known theologians are to be found especially within the Evangelical Theology group of the American Academy of Religion. Even the Evangelical Theological Society, which in recent years has chosen its officers exclusively from the most conservative wing of the society, now has a number of younger members who represent the postconservative element.

# 2 The Task and Method of Theology

**Understanding** a theology begins with understanding its conception of its task and how it goes about accomplishing that task—in other words, theological prolegomena and methodology. In this chapter, we examine four different programs of theological methodology that can be classified as representing the evangelical left, or postconservative evangelicalism.

One thing that can be clearly seen in these several approaches is a concern with the modern world, or with the Enlightenment. Postconservatives believe a profound change took place in the world with the coming of the Enlightenment, a change that must be taken into account in doing theology in our time, if that theology is to be truly a responsible theology. They therefore see the task of theology as in large part consisting of a response to this historical development. Just how that response is made will vary from one to another.

## Types of Responses

*Bernard Ramm.* The development and change in Bernard Ramm's thought are interesting. At one point, he was a staunch defender of the received or traditional conservative doctrines. He was especially oriented to apologetics. Probably his major work of this period, and perhaps of his entire writing career, was his *Christian View of Science and Scripture.*[1] With a background in science and a specialty in philosophy of

1. Bernard Ramm, *The Christian View of Science and Scripture* (Grand Rapids: Eerdmans, 1955).

science in his doctoral program, he naturally was concerned with the relationship of science to theology and scriptural revelation. In his book, he argued for a harmony of general revelation and special revelation, when a sufficient induction of the sources is conducted and those sources are properly interpreted. He did not follow the most literal hermeneutics with respect to the passages in question, but pursued a basically conservative approach to Scripture. In *Protestant Christian Evidences*, he had argued from such traditional concerns as fulfilled prophecy, miracle, archaeology, and the popularity and influence of the Bible, for a very conventional conception of that authority.[2] His *Protestant Biblical Interpretation* presupposed a propositional view of revelation.[3] His *Pattern of Religious Authority*[4] and his *Special Revelation and the Word of God*[5] presupposed and defended a propositional view of revelation as the communication of divine truth. At a number of points, he was quite critical of Karl Barth's methodology and view of revelation.[6]

Although a number of factors served to bring about changes in Ramm's views, he attributes the precipitating impulse to a particular incident when he was lecturing on the methodology of his version of evangelical theology. A listener asked for a more precise definition of evangelical theology. Suddenly Ramm, in an experience similar to that of a drowning person, saw his theology pass before his eyes. He realized that what he had was a collection of doctrines picked up over the years in various places, but that he did not really have a comprehensive theological methodology. Upon further reflection, he concluded that theologically he was the product of the orthodox–

2. Bernard Ramm, *Protestant Christian Evidences: A Textbook of the Evidences of the Truthfulness of the Christian Faith for Conservative Protestants* (Chicago: Moody, 1953).

3. Bernard Ramm, *Protestant Biblical Interpretation: A Textbook of Hermeneutics for Conservative Protestants* (Boston: W. A. Wilde, 1950).

4. Bernard Ramm, *The Pattern of Religious Authority* (Grand Rapids: Eerdmans, 1959).

5. Bernard Ramm, *Special Revelation and the Word of God* (Grand Rapids: Eerdmans, 1961).

6. *The Pattern of Religious Authority*, pp. 91–101.

liberal debate that had been going on for a century, and that it had warped evangelical theology.[7]

The attempt to overcome this distortion and to develop a thoroughgoing evangelical theology apart from that controversy now began to occupy Ramm's attention. He had been exposed to Karl Barth's thought earlier, but now began studying it in earnest, as well as that of the Dutch Reformed theologian, Abraham Kuyper. A sabbatical leave enabled him to go to Basel to study with Barth. Out of this study and reflection came a rather remarkable recommendation, enunciated in the book *After Fundamentalism*.

For Ramm, then, the question that concerns evangelical theological methodology most at the present time is the question of how it is to be related to the Enlightenment, which occurred in the eighteenth century but with effects still felt today. The Enlightenment represented the radical secularization of European culture. It rejected authority of any kind external to the individual, but especially the authority of the church. Reason, freedom, rights, and happiness were among the words designating the desired values. Among the terms that represented the undesirable qualities were authority, antiquity, tradition, and the like. The state, formerly understood as divinely instituted and sanctioned, was now interpreted rather as a social contract. This was the period in which appeal to some theological authority to settle a matter was replaced by the use of science to get at the truth. Whatever is claimed as truth must justify itself before the bar of reason. All ideas and all claimed historical documents must be submitted to the scrutiny of historical and literary criticism. This was naturalism—the belief that reality is basically limited to observable nature, and humanism—the conception that humanity is the highest form of reality within the universe, and the measure of all things.[8]

In many ways, the Enlightenment was a renewal and a heightening of the emphases that arose during the Renaissance. There was one major difference, however, according to Ramm. Whereas the Renaissance had been a movement within

---

7. Bernard Ramm, *After Fundamentalism: The Future of Evangelical Theology* (San Francisco: Harper and Row, 1983), p. 1.

8. Ibid., pp. 2–5.

the church, the Enlightenment moved outside the church, presenting alternatives and threats to the church and its teachings.[9] Ramm found that he had to revise his understanding of church history, specifically, the history of theology. He had previously held that Schleiermacher was the founder of theological liberalism, and that departures from orthodoxy on a large scale basically began in this period. Now, however, he found that a group of innovators, the Neologians in the eighteenth century, had already upset Protestant orthodox theology. What they had begun in the middle of the eighteenth century had been carried out even more vigorously by the rationalists in the latter half of that century.[10]

There were various attempts to construct a view of religion and even a theology in light of these considerations. One was deism, which basically concluded that the older orthodoxy simply could not be maintained. A religion whose tenets could meet the scrutiny of reason must be adopted instead. This would be a rational religion, common to all persons and involving the spirit of tolerance. Similarly, Kant had argued in his *Critique of Pure Reason* that it is impossible to have rational or theoretical knowledge of any objects that transcend sensory experience. The attempt to construct such leads one to antinomies, or two opposed but mutually plausible alternatives on any of several major topics. Instead, Kant maintained, God must be reintroduced as a guarantor of moral values and actions. Religion, then, according to Kant, became a matter of practice or of ethics. Albrecht Ritschl, accepting Kant's argument, concluded that religion is a matter of value judgments rather than judgments of factuality.

One early attempt to form an alternative response to the Enlightenment was made by Friedrich Schleiermacher. He accepted the Enlightenment critique of orthodox theology, which could no longer be maintained. On the other hand, however, he rejected deism as well as Kant's religious philosophy, which distorted the true nature of religion. He decided that a third approach would be more successful, by drawing on a philosophy that was popular at his time, romanticism. He concluded that

9. Ibid., pp. 3–4.
10. Ibid., pp. 5–6.

religion was not a matter of knowing, as orthodoxy had thought, or of doing, as Kant had argued. Rather, it was a matter of feeling, especially the feeling of absolute dependence.[11]

Ramm does not find Schleiermacher's response to the Enlightenment an acceptable option. But if the Enlightenment eliminated the possibility of the orthodox view for the intelligentsia, and if liberalism is a result of an attempted response to the Enlightenment, then the Enlightenment must be taken seriously but not capitulated to. There must be another option that evangelicalism can follow.

Ramm sought for this in the theology of Karl Barth, and was pleased with what he found. Studying with Barth in Basel and reading extensively in his works, Ramm encountered some surprises. The Barth that he had heard depicted by theologians of both a conservative and a liberal stripe was not really the Barth that he encountered in person and in his writings.[12] One day, while Ramm was lecturing on the Enlightenment and explaining to his class that nineteenth- and twentieth-century theologies could be classified by how they reacted to the Enlightenment, the thought came to him that Barth's theology was a restatement of Reformed theology, written in response to the Enlightenment but not capitulating to it.[13] He notes three elements in Barth's theological program:

1. He rejected the Neologians' criticism of historic Christian orthodoxy.
2. He accepted the positive accomplishments of the Enlightenment.
3. He rewrote his Reformed theology in the light of the Enlightenment.[14]

Ramm says that Barth is not for everyone. He is, however, for those who believe that the Enlightenment has precipitated a crisis for evangelical theology, the best option available. Barth's method can be used by a five-point Calvinist, a five-

11. Ibid., pp. 6–8.
12. Ibid., pp. 22–25.
13. Ibid., p. 13.
14. Ibid., p. 14.

point Arminian, a five-point fundamentalist, and a seven-point dispensationalist.[15]

Much of Ramm's book consists of defending Barth against the criticisms he has received from various sources. His most common method of defense is to contend that these, whether from the right or the left, have simply not understood Barth correctly. He then goes on to show how Barth's method led him to conclusions in areas such as Scripture[16] and salvation[17] that were different from the fundamentalist obscurantist response. Nonetheless, Barth preserved the content of orthodoxy while taking the Enlightenment into account, but not capitulating to it.

What is amazing about Ramm's adoption and defense of Barth's methodology is that he never, in this reader's judgment, tells us just what that method is. He makes certain predications about it, such as that it was a preservation of Reformed theology and that it took the Enlightenment into account, and shows the result of that method, but he really never defines the method. Thus, one is left wondering, at the end, how to apply Barth's method, rather than simply accepting the results of that method.

*Clark Pinnock.* Pinnock begins his discussion with an examination of the present condition in theology. Before doing even that, however, he asks the reader's question: Why should we even be concerned about theology? This is not an uncommon objection, especially within the evangelical community. Pinnock contends for the importance of theology because of three functions that it performs:[18]

1. The ecclesial function. Theology is a study of what Christians believe and confess, the vision that sustains the community. The New Testament warns of the danger of exchanging the truth of God for a lie. Theology calls the church to fidelity to God, because the church's health and strength depend on this.

15. Ibid., p. 28.
16. Ibid., pp. 88–134.
17. Ibid., pp. 165–72.
18. Clark Pinnock, *Tracking the Maze: Finding Our Way Through Modern Theology from an Evangelical Perspective* (San Francisco: Harper and Row, 1990), pp. 3–7.

2. The societal function. Christians are called to be salt and light in the world. There has been an increasing understanding of what Pinnock calls "social sanctification"—the transformation of society. This is particularly important in our time, when the failure of secular solutions to society's problems is so obvious.
3. The missiological function. At its best, theology emphasizes the role of the church in taking the message of salvation to the world. Unfortunately, theology often has stressed the church as a turned-in or ghettoized existence.

Pinnock observes that the theological scene today is a confused one. In trying to sort out the various types of theology, he sees them in terms of the attempt to relate the core of the Christian message to the modern world. There are three basic types of response. The progressives stress bringing the message up to date, so that it connects with contemporary experience. In so doing, they are willing to modify the past forms of theology. The conservatives, on the other hand, emphasize the preservation of the revelation, even if that puts theology at odds with modern culture at some points. Finally, the moderates are those who feel uncomfortable with either of these alternatives, and try to strike a balance between text and context.[19]

The remainder of part 1 is devoted to elaborating these three responses. Examples of the progressives Pinnock cites include Don Cupitt, Lonnie Kliever, Gordon Kaufman, Edward Farley, John Hick, Ben Smillie, Rosemary Ruether, Schubert Ogden, Rudolf Bultmann, and Paul Tillich. Examples of the conservative approach are found in traditional Catholicism and in Protestantism (the Old Princeton school, Cornelius Van Til, Carl F. H. Henry). One of the most interesting points he makes is the similarity of Protestant conservatives to Catholic conservatives, involving the role of tradition and the infallible church.[20] Pinnock divides the moderates into postliberals and postconservatives. The former include the neoorthodox, Wolfhart Pannenberg, George Lindbeck, Geoffrey Wainwright, Peter Berger,

19. Ibid., pp. 11–14.
20. Ibid., pp. 38–42.

and Thomas Oden. Under the latter he mentions Vatican II and evangelicalism. Interestingly, he does not name any individuals among postconservative evangelicals. He does list several characteristics of this group, however:[21]

1. More openness to the humanity of the Bible, and consequently, greater acceptance of biblical criticism.
2. Recognition of the diversity within the Bible, and consequently, greater tolerance for theological pluralism within their ranks.
3. New respect for the value of tradition, especially in a time of considerable change.
4. Open discussion about the deity and God's openness to the temporal process.
5. Greater willingness to consider evolution as a complementary explanation of origins.
6. In salvation, a move away from double predestination; the possibility of salvation of the unevangelized on the basis of the light they have or of a postmortem encounter; an openness to annihilation, rather than hell as endless suffering of the lost.
7. A greater openness to the idea of Christ transforming culture, resulting in something of an evangelical social gospel or liberation theology.
8. A greater willingness to accept the idea of the occurrence of miracles today.
9. An evangelical ecumenism, working cooperatively with all who confess evangelical doctrine.

This leads Pinnock to a more extensive examination of the phenomenon of modernity. This was a radical shift from the medieval worldview with its emphasis on God and the authority of his revelation. Instead, modernity involved a radical anthropocentrism or humanism, with humans fully capable of discovering and understanding the truth themselves. This was the result of developments in science, philosophy, psychology, and biblical criticism. Pinnock describes the thought of three precursors of the modernist movement (Descartes, Locke, and

21. Ibid., pp. 67–68.

Hume) and then the modernist tide (Kant, Schleiermacher, and Hegel). He shows the resistance and reaction offered by Kierkegaard, Bultmann, Barth and Brunner, and evangelicalism, and the resurgence of liberalism, in the form of the death of God theology.

This brings Pinnock to the all important question of what is to be done in the present situation. He begins with a discussion of a question that was frequently addressed in the nineteenth century, but which, in my judgment, is indispensible in the present situation: What is the essence of Christianity? Without having systematically addressed this question, we may either fail to preserve that which is essential or find ourselves defending more than we need to. Pinnock believes that the essence of the gospel is the biblically narrated epic story of salvation through Jesus Christ.[22] He asks, "What is the heart of the Christian revelation, then? It is that God himself in grace has broken through into history and human culture. The gospel proclamation is like a newscast, announcing what God has done for the salvation of humankind, how that God has come in the life, death and Resurrection of Jesus Christ to reveal to us our true condition and to effect our reconciliation."[23] It is based on historical fact, but fact that has application and significance for all persons. It is more than fact without being less. It is myth become fact.[24] The argument for the story is not primarily through a rational defense of its claims, however, but by showing its relevance to ordinary human experience.

Pinnock notes that revelation does not simply stand alone, but creates certain secondary forms of itself. These are the sources or authorities that Pinnock will utilize. Revelation is presupposed in them all: "it occurs and finds itself recorded in sacred writings, passed down through the generations, all the while eliciting a richness of experiential responses and rational reflections."[25] So he treats, in turn, Scripture, tradition, experience, and reason—the familiar Wesleyan quadrilateral of authority.

22. Ibid., p. 154.
23. Ibid., p. 158.
24. Ibid., p. 164.
25. Ibid., p. 171.

1. Scripture. The authority of the Scripture rests especially in its bearing witness to the story of what God has done and is doing for us. It is important that we see the Bible's center of gravity as being the salvation story, rather than the perfection of the text as a document.[26] Pinnock makes the point that inspiration, strictly speaking, would not have been necessary. The truth of the gospel rests on what Christ has done, whether there is an inspired record of that or not. Nonetheless, we do hold to inspiration for two reasons. One is that there are indications that God has indeed inspired the Bible. Throughout it we find statements treating it as being the documentation of God's revelation. Further, there is a certain logic at work. If the revelation is to benefit others beside its initial recipients, there needs to be a means of preserving it, beyond the vagaries of merely oral repetition of the story.[27]

The understanding of Scripture that we now have enables us to see its full humanity. This will prevent us from simply proof texting without regard for the context and nature of the texts. We will be conscious that the Scriptures are not all of the same nature. There are elements in them that derive from the culture of the writers, not from revelation.[28]

2. Tradition. This carries the event of revelation forward. It means that we are members of a community, and are not making an individual statement when we say we believe. "The community transmits the Word down through time, helps the faithful to understand it, and tries to locate the relevance of the biblical message for each new situation."[29]

3. Experience. This is where our own encounters with God can be added to the experiences and recollections of the historical community. Ideally, our own experiences will be in agreement with those of the community or the tradition. In personal experience, the received message becomes personally real and confirmed.[30]

4. Reason. In Anselmian fashion, Pinnock sees faith as seeking understanding, and this is where reason enters in. This in-

---

26. Ibid., pp. 171–72.
27. Ibid., pp. 173–74.
28. Ibid., p. 176.
29. Ibid., p. 177.
30. Ibid., p. 178.

volves critical analysis, in order to avoid internal contradiction, the incorporation of new scientific, historical, and experiential data, and the working out of the systematic dimensions of the Christian faith. Reason must always serve a ministerial rather than a magisterial role. It does not sit in final judgment as to the truth of matters, but assists in understanding itself, all the while respecting the dimension of mystery in the Christian faith and the limitations of reason.[31]

Pinnock then addresses more definitively the question of the nature of theology. He contrasts narrative theology, which is what he is attempting, with the older approach of propositional theology. Theology, he asserts, is a second-level endeavor. Theologians have often made the mistake of ignoring the narrative form of revelation and trying to turn doctrine into propositions. This assumes that people are primarily rational. Stories are treated almost as illustratory of the main point, the proposition. Yet stories are dynamic and invite the reader or hearer to enter into them in ways that propositions do not.[32]

Theology, then, has the task, not of translating stories into abstract propositions, but of exploring and proclaiming the Christian story. Theology is evaluated in terms of the effectiveness with which its doctrines do this: "Doctrines that help us understand the story better are good and true; doctrines that ruin and distort the story are false and harmful." Similarly, Pinnock says, "We should redefine heresy as something that ruins the story and orthodoxy as something that keeps the story alive and devises new ways of telling it. Within this kind of theology, there will be room for liberal Christians to relate contemporary stories and for conservative Christians to rehearse the mighty deeds of God."[33]

The contrast between propositional theology and narrative theology can be seen as follows. Propositional theology forms concepts and asks for an intellectual response, whereas narrative theology proclaims good news, builds systems, and stimulates debate over concepts. Narrative theology, on the other hand, proclaims the Good News of Christ, and thinks about

31. Ibid., pp. 178–79.
32. Ibid., pp. 182–83.
33. Ibid., p. 183.

how to express it and live it; it tells stories that cannot be completely captured in logical systems; rather than spurring debate, it evokes participation and following of Christ. It integrates knowing and doing better than propositional theology.[34]

This approach would seem to present a problem, which Pinnock recognizes and addresses: How does one identify heresy? When doctrine was thought of as propositions, this was a fairly easy question to answer, but what about this narrative approach? If heresy, or at least unsound theology, is that which distorts the story, how does one decide what is a distortion of the story? Does this not presuppose some official interpretation of the story? This, however, is not as problematic as it may appear, for the story is not simply uninterpreted. While it is important to agree on the major features of the story, the community should be able to allow disagreement on some of the details. Among these Pinnock mentions the question of whether God should ever be addressed as mother, God's knowledge of all future contingencies, infant baptism, eternal hell, and election of some to salvation and others to damnation. These questions should be left unsettled, rather than breaking fellowship over them.[35]

To illustrate this point, Pinnock then walks through the various stages of the story and shows the distortions that have been introduced into the story by various theologies. Thus, Augustine's doctrine that God planned the damnation of the damned was a distortion of the prologue; confusing the creation account of Genesis 1 with scientific description or viewing it as myth and not event has distorted the beginning of the story; classical theism has distorted the picture of the relationship of God and his human covenant partner by picturing God as immutable, not responding to human actions, and manipulating humanity, thus robbing human beings of freedom. Pinnock blames the more liberal theologies for distortion at the point of the incarnation and the resurrection of Jesus, but overall, his strongest and most numerous criticisms are directed at conservatives, especially Augustine, who transformed the doctrine of the election of the nation of Israel to service into a doc-

34. Ibid., pp. 184–85.
35. Ibid., pp. 189–90.

trine of double predestination of individuals, to either salvation or damnation.[36]

*Stanley Grenz.* In some ways more radical than Pinnock and Ramm is Stanley Grenz in his *Revisioning Evangelical Theology*. As the title indicates, he is calling for a new approach to doing theology. He begins, however, with the definition of evangelicalism. To understand contemporary evangelicalism it is necessary to examine its history. It has come to its present form through three historical waves. The first was the Reformation, the second was Puritanism and Pietism, and the third was the post-fundamentalist, "card-carrying" evangelicalism. This latter group was the "new evangelicalism" pioneered by Harold John Ockenga and others, and largely grew out of the rancorous dispute known as the fundamentalist–modernist controversy. The new evangelicals wanted to learn from the mistakes of their fundamentalist forebears, and consequently, they stood between the liberal and fundamentalist factions and approaches. They were more inclined to engagement with the world and to dialogue with those who were not evangelical in their theology. Yet their theological orientation was profoundly affected by that dispute. Because the debate was largely in terms of theology, evangelicalism tended to define itself as a theological movement, embodied in lists of doctrinal tenets. This was in contrast to the nineteenth century, when evangelicalism was defined more in terms of a personal relationship to God. Especially, the doctrine of Scripture was hardened into belief in inerrancy.[37]

Grenz contends, however, that an examination of evangelicalism's history indicates that this definition in terms of theological position is too narrow. This new evangelicalism or card-carrying evangelicalism is only one expression of evangelicalism, not its sole, authentic form. Rather, evangelical identity is something that is really sensed more than described. It is in terms of a particular spirituality. This involves a desire to see the Bible come alive in one's personal experience and in community life. There is a sense that faith should be a vibrant part of life. There is an approach to worship that centers on praise

36. Ibid., pp. 191–210.
37. Ibid., pp. 22–29.

and experience of God, especially through singing. There is a common way of understanding oneself in terms of a story or narrative, of having been lost and then saved. This experience takes place within a biblical and theological context, of course. There is a reciprocal relationship between the experience and the doctrines. The doctrines grow out of the experience, but they also shape the experience. In the final analysis, although evangelicalism involves doctrines, it is much more than mere theology. Grenz says, "the ethos of evangelicalism in any generation and in any expression . . . is an experiential piety cradled in a theology."[38]

This spirituality emphasizes the inward personal experience of God, as found in the new birth and continued in the emphasis on spiritual growth. Abstract doctrine is not enough. Evangelicals emphasize that doctrine must be experienced personally. Its purpose is the production of spirituality in the believer.[39]

This brings Grenz to the understanding of the theological task. Here he stakes out his ground by contrasting the revisioned approach with a more traditional form of evangelicalism. He quotes Klaus Bockmuehl's description of the task of systematic theology as representative of the evangelicals who see theology as systematizing the doctrine found in Scripture: "to produce a summary of Christian doctrine, an ordered summary or synopsis of the themes of teaching in Holy Scripture. We are to collect the different, dispersed propositions on essential themes or topics of the OT and the NT and put them together in an order that fits the subject-matter at hand."[40] While this may sound like a standard definition to many evangelicals, Grenz demurs: "Although it rightly seeks to uphold the authority of the Bible, this approach cannot serve as a catalyst for a revisioned evangelical theology."[41]

38. Stanley J. Grenz, *Revisioning Evangelical Theology: A Fresh Agenda for the 21st Century* (Downers Grove, Ill.: InterVarsity, 1993), p. 35.

39. Ibid., p. 57.

40. Klaus Bockmuehl, "The Task of Systematic Theology," in *Perspectives on Evangelical Theology*, ed. Kenneth S. Kantzer and Stanley N. Gundry (Grand Rapids: Baker, 1979), p. 4. Quoted in Grenz, *Revisioning*, p. 62.

41. Grenz, *Revisioning*, p. 62.

Like Pinnock, Grenz is critical of the propositional approach to revelation and theology. Although the method of biblical summarization has a strong historical pedigree, it has come under attack by liberals and the neoorthodox. While some evangelicals have called for a contextualization of the propositional truth, others have insisted that this did not go far enough. What Grenz proposes in its place is a narrative approach, the narrative of God's working within history. This means that theology can only be done from within the faith community.[42] This approach is also consistent with the new understanding of the formation of the canon.

What, then, is the specific understanding of the theological task that Grenz is proposing instead of the older propositional approach to biblical summarization? He states it several times: "In the broad sense, then, we may define systematic theology as the intellectual reflection on the act, and the attempt to articulate the content, of Christian faith, including its expression in beliefs, practices, and institutions."[43] "Theology, in contrast, is the believing community's intellectual reflection on faith."[44] "A revisioned evangelical theology seeks to reflect on the faith commitment of the believing community in order to construct a model of reality."[45] The distinction of his understanding of the task of theology is between the older idea of theology as biblical summarization and this conception of theology as reflection on the faith commitment of the believing community. Here, Roger Olson observes,[46] Grenz is explicitly agreeing with postliberal George Lindbeck's definition of doctrine.[47]

The final aspect of Grenz's program that we wish to examine in this chapter is his revisioning of the sources of evangelical theology. Traditionally, evangelicalism has claimed to limit this to one source, the Bible. Grenz again describes this approach and his attitude toward it: "Evangelical theologians

42. Ibid., p. 72.
43. Ibid, p. 64.
44. Ibid., p. 81.
45. Ibid., p. 85.
46. Roger E. Olson, "Whales and Elephants: Both God's Creatures But Can They Meet?" *Pro Ecclesia* 4.2 (Spring 1995): 180.
47. George A. Lindbeck, *The Nature of Doctrine: Religion and Theology in a Postliberal Age* (Philadelphia: Westminster, 1984).

ought to move away from conceiving their task as merely to discover divinely revealed truth understood as the single, doctrinal system purportedly lodged within the pages of Scripture and waiting to be categorized and systematized."[48] There seems to be some ambiguity in Grenz's statement, within a single sentence, over whether the view is that a system of doctrine already exists within Scripture, waiting to be discovered, or whether it is merely the raw material from which a system is to be developed. In any event, while granting the need for some systematization, Grenz says that the emphasis must be on the distinctively practical aspect of doctrine.[49]

Some evangelicals, such as Clark Pinnock, have adopted the Wesleyan quadrilateral (Scripture, tradition, experience, and reason). Grenz is quite critical of any approach that seeks to utilize experience as a theological source. He especially objects to the use of experience as a norm for theology separate from the others, rather than as a medium of its reception. The difficulty, as he sees it, is that experience never comes in uninterpreted form. Besides that, individual experience inevitably tends to be rather subjective in nature and to lack universalizability. Having said that, however, he finds experience informative, for it helps clarify our relationship to God.[50]

Grenz proposes three sources of theology, or three norms, since he equates source and norm. The first, as we might well expect, is the Bible. This does not, however, require the construction of any elaborate prolegomenon to theology, in which the legitimacy of appeal to the Scriptures is established. We may accept it simply because it is the universally acknowledged book of the Christian church, the central norm for the articulation of the faith of the community.[51] We cannot, however, simply leap from the repetition of the Bible's contents to the present time. Guidance in this task requires the use of a secondary authority, the theological heritage of the church. This is really an extension of the first norm, since it is a product of the church's continuing reflection on the

48. Ibid., p. 88.
49. Ibid.
50. Ibid., pp. 91–93.
51. Ibid., pp. 93–94.

message. We can learn from the past some of the pitfalls into which the church can fall, but also can learn positively from what those theologians did in relating the message to their time. Beyond that, however, there are certain formulations that have stood the test of time. These confessions and creeds must of course be tested against the primary norm, the Scriptures, but are nonetheless valuable.[52]

Grenz's third norm is in some ways perhaps the most surprising, at least in the way in which it is stated. This is the thought forms of contemporary culture. To be relevant, the church must fashion its message in terms of those thought forms. The culture will give us guidance regarding the issues to be explored. Beyond that, however, "it also functions in demarcating the ways theologians handle these issues."[53] The church has always done its theology in a particular historical-cultural setting, as when it used Greek metaphysical categories to express the doctrine of the incarnation. As further illustration, Grenz contends that Anselm replaced the ransom theory of the atonement with the satisfaction theory in a feudalistic society, and then when national governments succeeded feudalism, the substitutionary-penal theory replaced the satisfaction theory.[54]

These three norms should not be thought of as functioning independently of one another, but as being used together in proper balance. Different theologies tend to emphasize one of these to the neglect of the others, fundamentalists keying in on the first, confessionalists the second, and progressives the third. There is no question about the role of culture in Grenz's theology.[55] Yet he warns against the danger of becoming too accommodated to culture, which in our time is in some ways a greater danger for evangelicals than for liberals.[56]

52. Ibid., pp. 94–97.
53. Ibid., p. 98.
54. Ibid., p. 99.
55. Timothy R. Phillips and Dennis L. Okholm observe that "these statements [by Grenz regarding the norm of culture] cannot be explained as careless speech." "The Nature of Confession: Evangelicals and Postliberals," in *The Nature of Confession: Evangelicals and Postliberals in Conversation*, ed. Timothy R. Phillips and Dennis L. Okholm (Downers Grove, Ill.: InterVarsity, 1996), p. 8, n. 6.
56. Grenz, *Revisioning*, pp. 107–8.

*James McClendon.* Until recently, McClendon would not have been labeled an evangelical. For the past several years, McClendon, together with his wife, Nancey Murphy, has taught at Fuller Seminary, which qualifies him for inclusion in this theological movement.

An essential starting point for McClendon's thought is that theology must now be done within a different milieu than even two decades ago. This is evidenced by his prefaces to revised editions of two of his books.[57] A significant cultural and intellectual paradigm shift is taking place, from the modern to the postmodern period, and this shift is in part what has occasioned and required the revision of the earlier articles. With Murphy he describes modernity by displaying it along three axes: an epistemological axis running between foundationalism and skepticism; a linguistic axis running between representationalism and expressivism; and an axis running between individualism and collectivism.[58] They then "propose to define as postmodern any mode of thought that departs from the three modern axes described above without reverting to premodern categories."[59]

Whereas the theology of the most recent period had been done in modern categories, McClendon is attempting to do theology in a postmodern fashion. This can be seen, for example, in his and Smith's discussion of religious language. Whereas in the modern period this had been pursued within the axis in which language must either be representative of some extralinguistic object or expressive of subjective feelings, they explore as a further possibility the speech-act theory of religious language propounded by John L. Austin. Here one regards speech as a type of action, and asks of an utterance, "What does it do?" They note that in "telling" someone something, I may be advising, or ordering, or objecting.[60] In practice, the representative,

---

57. "Preface to the New Edition," *Biography as Theology: How Life Stories Can Remake Theology* (Philadephia: Trinity, 1990), pp. v–xi; "Preface to the Revised Edition," *Convictions: Defusing Religious Relativism* [with James M. Smith] (Valley, Forge, Pa.: Trinity, 1994), pp. ix–x.

58. Nancey Murphy and James William McClendon Jr., "Distinguishing Modern and Postmodern Theologies," *Modern Theology* 5.3 (April 1989): 191–98.

59. Ibid., p. 199.

60. McClendon and Smith, *Convictions*, p. 53.

primary, and affective elements of utterances are so inter-twined that determining what is true is an elusive matter. We are here dealing with convictions, and we must ask what makes convictions justifiable.[61]

There is another way of coming at the issue of theological method, and that is by noting the parallel between theology and ethics. Because the changes in theology, away from the old landmarks of Barth, Rahner, Tillich, and Congar, are part of a shift in the general mood, it is instructive to observe the changes effected in another discipline by this change in mood.[62]

When McClendon surveys the scene in ethics, he observes that the prevailing approach for some years was utilitarianism, which attempted to determine what was the greatest good for the greatest number.[63] The proposed alternatives to this, such as situationism and principle-based ethics, were similarly attempt-ing to identify the right course of action. They all seem to regard that as, in a sense, person-independent. Joseph Fletcher, for ex-ample, in his discussion of mothers and their decision whether to kill their crying babies to prevent them from betraying the presence of the entire group, does not really ask about what the mothers were like, or what the group of which they were a part was like. In contrast to what he calls quandary-ethics, he be-lieves that in the changed situation, a character ethics will be more adequate.[64] Here, having character, being a person of character, is a precondition of making moral choices.[65] This is what distinguishes a truly moral act from an otherwise identi-cal act by someone who does it merely out of whim or from a selfish motive.

This matter of character is not to be thought of in too indi-vidualistic a fashion, however. It would be better to speak of character-in-community, for communities also have charac-ters, which acknowledges "the reference of character to the human setting that fosters and recognizes it. This can be seen clearly if we recognize that communities have their own dis-

---

61. Ibid., p. 78.
62. *Biography as Theology*, p. 1.
63. Ibid., p. 2.
64. Ibid., p. 14.
65. Ibid., p. 15.

tinctive characters, and that signs of this distinctive character are the community's holding certain convictions—the same convictions that inform and give shape to many individual members of the community."[66]

There are, then, ethical convictions, but there are also theological convictions, although McClendon would not separate these two sharply. This leads him to his definition of doctrine: "Christian beliefs are not so many 'propositions' to be catalogued or juggled like truth-functions in a computer, but are living convictions which give shape to actual lives in actual communities."[67] Christianity turns on the character of Christ. We must, however, find fresh exemplars of that character, lest it be consigned to antiquarian lore. Thus, the study of persons who to an outstanding degree embody that character is an important function of theology in this new environment.[68]

Here is a major contrast between biographical theology and propositional theology. For propositional theology, the object is the abstract concepts presented in the Bible, even if that message of the Bible is transformed for the present age. "For a biographical theology (although it acknowledges that the lives it attends to each incorporate convictions), the center must be the lives themselves, or more accurately must be one life, *the life of Christ*."[69] Crucial to this statement is a distinction between the life of Jesus, the man who lived in first-century Palestine, and the life of Christ, who rose and lives in his community, in the world. We cannot develop a full-fledged conservative "life of Jesus," as some have attempted in the past, complete with chronology. But, following Conzelmann,[70] McClendon believes that although we cannot formulate a portrait of Jesus, we can learn what his character was.[71] Unlike the life of Jesus, however, which ended in the first century, the life of Christ is a continuing matter, for he lives on in the community,

66. Ibid., p. 17.
67. Ibid., p. 22.
68. Ibid., p. 23.
69. Ibid., pp. 166–67.
70. Hans Conzelmann, *Jesus*, trans. J. Raymond Lord (Philadelphia: Fortress, 1973).
71. McClendon, *Biography*, p. 169. It should be noted that McClendon apparently accepts the now much disputed "principle of dissimilarity" (p. 168).

which is the church. McClendon gives as a major justification for the study of biography:

> Out of death Christ arose. The shared life which is oriented to and grows from that new fact is continuous with the solitary life of Jesus (it is *Jesus* Christ who rose from the dead); yet it possesses a fibrous dimension of breadth that the single thread of Jesus' life does not (it is Jesus *Christ* who arose). That solitary thread is now the shared life of those whom he redeems. They are in Christ; Christ is in them (Gal. 1:22; Rom. 8:10). The life of Christ cannot be told without the whole New Testament, without the whole history of the "God movement," without the whole human story *annis domini*—in the years of the Lord. In this sense, the lives of the saints significantly participate in the life of Christ; telling their stories is a part of telling *the* story.[72]

## Analysis of the Movement

We have sampled four postconservative proposals for doing theology for our time. Several analytical observations need to be made, based on these and other representative statements:

1. There is a profound recognition of the impact that the Enlightenment has made on the situation in which theology is to be done. Many recent theological movements can be understood by reference to their response to this major development.
2. There is a strong sense of the importance of expressing theology in a contemporary fashion, in order to make it relevant to the needs of persons.
3. There is a multiple-source approach to methodology. Rather than restricting theology to the use of one source, the Bible, as evangelicalism has done in an earlier time, this type of evangelicalism sees it as one, although generally the primary, source of its theology.
4. There is a confession of the historically conditioned character of all theology, indeed of the contents of all disciplines. The implications of this fact are not ordinarily spelled out in any detail, however.

72. Ibid., pp. 169–70.

5. There is an overall rejection of foundationalism. By this is meant what I sometimes term "hard foundationalism"—the idea that there are certain indubitable starting points on which thought may proceed. There is, however, an acceptance of "soft foundationalism," the idea that there is objective truth whether we can demonstrate its reality conclusively.[73]

6. In general, there is a stronger reliance on experience than in most earlier evangelicalism. This is most prominent in the thought of Pinnock and those closely associated with him.

7. There is a stronger emphasis on human freedom in these theologies than in the evangelicalism that produced the major theological work of the nineteenth and twentieth centuries. In some cases, this is similar to traditional Arminianism; in other cases, it goes well beyond the place of free will in Arminian theology.

8. There is a willingness to engage in dialogue with those of a more liberal orientation. Such dialogue is not primarily intended to convince these dialogue partners of the correctness of the evangelical way, or simply to inform the other. There is belief that something of benefit to the evangelical theologian can be acquired from the more liberal person.[74]

9. The evangelicalism of the immediately preceding generation, often regarded as "establishment evangelicalism" or "card-carrying evangelicalism," is considered to be just one historically conditioned form of evangelicalism, when compared to the whole sweep of evangelical thought throughout history and various cultures. It

73. Murphy and McClendon seem not to recognize any distinction such as this. Their description of foundationalism is of the former variety, but the fashion in which they present their description seems to assume an objectivity such as is involved in soft foundationalism. "Distinguishing Modern and Postmodern Theologies," p. 192. Cf. David Clark's distinction between modernist foundationalism and epistemic foundationalism. "Relativism, Fideism, and the Promise of Postliberalism," in *The Nature of Confession: Evangelicals and Postliberals in Conversation*, ed. Timothy R. Phillips and Dennis L. Okholm (Downers Grove, Ill.: InterVarsity, 1996), pp. 114–16.

74. Roger E. Olson, "Whales and Elephants," pp. 165–89.

is especially believed to be colored by the fundamentalist–modernist controversy through which its preceding generation passed. This has produced an excessive concern with correct doctrine.

10. Propositional theology is regarded as producing a distortion of the true evangelical theological method. Narrative theology is believed to be closer to the nature of the biblical revelation itself, and to facilitate the actual application of the theology by the reader.

11. The human side of Scripture is given full force. There is an emphasis on the necessity of distinguishing between the different types of biblical statements, and treating each in a fashion appropriate to its nature, rather than simply proof-texting indiscriminately.

12. Measures of the adequacy of a given theological interpretation are frequently pragmatic, rather than exegetical, in nature.

13. The role of community as the context for doing theology is emphasized.

## Evaluation

How shall we assess these proposals for new methodology? There are both strengths and problems within this postconservative evangelical theological endeavor.

### Positive

1. These theologians have correctly recognized the conditioned nature of much thought. When and where we are born, what intellectual and religious traditions we are subjected to, have a great deal of influence on what we believe and how we articulate it.

2. There is a realization of the great difference that the Enlightenment made in the environment within which theology, or any other intellectual discipline, must be conducted.

3. There is realization that because of the essential limitations of each individual and the complexity of knowledge in our present time, theology must be a community endeavor.

4. There is a strong emphasis on the practical dimension of theology. Theology is not simply to be the accumulation and transmission of knowledge in its own right, but is to serve the purpose of enriching the spiritual life and building up the church.
5. The abstractions that have sometimes characterized theology are partly avoided by this theology.
6. The complex and varied nature of evangelicalism is recognized and accredited. Some of the relatively silent evangelicals of the previous generation have now begun to speak up and their insights are taken into account by postconservative evangelicals.
7. There is a genuine concern to avoid relativism and subjectivism, and to maintain the real objectivity of the Christian message.

### Negative

The method, perhaps because it is of fairly recent development, has a number of points of difficulty.

1. There is a lack of clarity about just how the method is used or even just what the method is. We observed this most clearly in the case of Ramm's recommendation of Barth's method, but it is also present in the narrative theology of Pinnock and Grenz. What is the difference between the traditional propositional theology and this narrative theology? Indeed, the theology is not really narrative theology, but perhaps, more correctly, "theology of narrative," for theology is a second-level activity and is in propositional rather than narrative form. Either that, or what Pinnock and Grenz are actually giving us is metatheology, the discussion of the method of theology, rather than theology itself, and it is this that is propositional. Some theologians of a more liberal persuasion actually tell stories, some of them contemporary, as the means of doing theology. What is the relationship between the stories of the Bible and the propositions of theology?

   Pinnock, to be sure, tells the Christian story in his book. If this, rather than the other chapters of the book, is what is really theology, however, the additional question becomes, just what distinguishes theology from preaching or teaching biblical content? Is the theologian not then in danger of dissolving systematic theology into biblical theology, a danger about which Grenz warned?[75] Grenz avoids this problem by making one of his norms contemporary culture, but it is not clear just how this is articulated with the story.

The undigested nature of the method seems most apparent when one examines Grenz's *Theology for the Community of God*, published a year after *Revisioning* and declared to be the execution of the agenda in the former.[76] It is not difficult to find the community theme in that book, but just how it is distinctly narrative rather than propositional theology is not so clear.

2. The most important question does not really get asked; indeed, it does not appear that these theologians even recognize it. That question takes various forms, but for our purposes, the question is, what is the nature of metatheological discourse? To put it differently, what sort of language is used in discussing various types of language, or what paradigm is being followed when one discusses paradigms and paradigm shifts? One would hope that McClendon and Smith would have dealt with this in their discussion of speech-act theory and religious language. They fail, however, to tell us what type of speech-act is involved in discussion of speech-act theory.[77]

3. If indeed what is being recommended is a narrative-based theology, rather than a truly narrative theology, then it appears that we are looking at a theology with considerable affinity to the "God who acts" type of theology of a generation ago. The freshness of this approach may be its relative newness within evangelicalism, rather than within theology in general. But it also suffers from one of the same problems that the "bibli-

---

75. Grenz, *Revisioning*, p. 102.

76. Stanley J. Grenz, *Theology for the Community of God* (Nashville: Broadman and Holman, 1994), p. x.

77. James William McClendon Jr. and James M. Smith, *Convictions: Defusing Religious Relativism* (Philadelphia: Trinity, 1994), pp. 47–79.

cal theology" movement contained. Simply, there are large portions of the Bible for which the idea of revelation as historical act does not really fit, as James Barr pointed out a generation ago.[78] Indeed, if one does a comparative analysis of the content of the Bible, the New Testament books that seem to deal most explicitly with narrative constitute only 56 to 62 percent of the content, depending on whether one treats Revelation as narrative. In the Old Testament, the narrative books (Genesis–Job) constitute 57 percent of the material. It can, of course, be argued that the prophetic books contain considerable narrative, which they surely do, or even that they represent interpretation of the narrative and that the narrative is an interpreted narrative. Then, however, the concept of narrative rather than proposition is being stretched considerably. And the poetical portions, which do not fit quite this easily within the structure, still present a problem—a point Barr made and that even G. Ernest Wright had to concede.[79]

4.  The representation of the evangelicalism of the establishment or card-carrying evangelicals is at times rather distorted. Grenz, for example, seems to contrast his understanding with the older evangelicalism on the grounds that, in his view, evangelicalism is not merely defined as doctrine. Interestingly, however, he does not document those statements with those from the other evangelicals in which they define evangelicalism as *merely* doctrine. Considerable rhetorical force is lent to the argument by this contrast, but the picture of the other view is not fully accurate.

    This appears also in the contention that the revisioned evangelical theology is different in insisting on theology issuing in practice, especially of the community. Interestingly, however, a survey of recent evangelical theology texts reveals that all of them insist on the

78. James Barr, "The Interpretation of Scripture. II. Revelation Through History in the Old Testament and in Modern Theology," *Interpretation* 17 (1963): 196–97.

79. G. Ernest Wright, *God Who Acts: Biblical Theology as Recital* (London: SCM, 1952), p. 103.

same thing. And certainly Carl F. H. Henry, who wrote extensively on ethics, saw ethics as deriving from theology. The older evangelicalism tends to distinguish ethics and devotional practice from theology, but not to separate them.

5. There is a clear and commendable declaration of the historically conditioned nature of theology. This, of course, must apply to their theology as well. What is disappointing is the lack of acknowledgment and perhaps even recognition of many of their own presuppositions. To someone thoroughly familiar with twentieth-century theology reading this theology and philosophy, unacknowledged presuppositions leap off the page. The functional conception of truth that is so often assumed derives ultimately from pragmatism. And there is considerable indebtedness to existentialism's view of subjective truth, which goes back to Kierkegaard. Indeed, the eclectic blending of these two streams may eventually prove to be a source of some difficulty for postconservatives. There is the familiar attribution of commonsense realism to the nineteenth-century Princeton theology's view of inspiration, but at least within these writings there is not a self-conscious defense of an alternative epistemology.

At points, the similarity to another philosophy or theology is so strong that documentation seems to be called for. Pinnock's contrast of propositional and narrative theology, for example, very closely follows that of Tilley.[80] Yet Tilley's presuppositions are not described or discussed. Does Pinnock share them or not?

---

80. Terrence Tilley, *Story Theology* (Wilmington, Del.: Michael Glazier, 1985), pp. 5–16.

# 3 The Doctrine of Scripture

**Of** the several doctrines, the one in which some departure from the established evangelical position first began to become apparent was the doctrine of Scripture. In fact, problems surfaced in that area twenty or more years before any of the other doctrines became problematic on any large scale. In part, this is because of the influences causing such difficulties. In the case of the doctrine of God, the problem has arisen largely from philosophical issues. With the doctrine of the extent of salvation, the difficulty stemmed from anthropological considerations, such as contact with persons professing religions other than Christianity. The doctrine of Scripture, however, came under particular pressure because of exegetical factors. Since evangelicals, by the very nature of their theology, have always strongly emphasized biblical studies, the problem considerations became more readily apparent here than in the other doctrines.

We observed in the opening chapter that one of the first signs of doctrinal diversity within the received evangelical community was the dispute that surfaced on "Black Saturday" at Fuller Seminary. The issue was whether the Bible was free from all error, particularly in terms of historical, geographical, and scientific factual references. Because Daniel Fuller was the one who initially raised the objection that sparked the controversy, his views became very significant in the subsequent discussions. The key to his view, and to his ability to continue to affirm biblical inerrancy, or at least, biblical infallibility, was a distinction between matters of faith and practice and matters of factual or empirical reference.

This distinction was developed further and argued at great length by the man who ultimately was Edward Carnell's successor in theology and philosophy of religion at Fuller, Jack Rogers. Rogers had received his doctorate at the Free University of Amsterdam in the Netherlands, where he studied with G. C. Berkouwer. Berkouwer in his book, *Holy Scripture*, revealed a theory of biblical authority and inspiration quite different from another branch of Reformed theology, the "Old Princeton" School. Rogers edited a book entitled *Biblical Authority*, which was intended to be at least a partial response to Harold Lindsell's *Battle for the Bible*. In his book, published in 1976, Lindsell sought to demonstrate the departures from belief in total inerrancy that had occurred within a number of denominations and schools, most notably, Fuller Seminary. Rogers contributed a chapter, "The Church Doctrine of Biblical Authority," to this volume, which he also edited.[1] The major thrust of the chapter was to contend that, rather than being the universal view of orthodox Christians down through the years of church history, the total inerrancy view was but one of several views and of rather recent origin. Rogers also collaborated with Donald McKim on a much larger work entitled *The Authority and Interpretation of the Bible in Historical Perspective*, which elaborated and documented this thesis at much greater length.

A number of arguments go into Rogers and McKim's volume, which will necessarily have to be summarized here in rather brief fashion. First, the early fathers did not hold to the idea of absolute inerrancy, in the sense of freedom from error in all matters the Bible addresses. Part of the argument is to cite indications from these Fathers that the biblical writers accommodated themselves in the expression of revealed truth. For example, Origen distinguished between the truth revealed to the biblical authors and their commentary on it. Further, Origen had received from the Alexandrian School a theory of the accommodation of eternal truth in Scripture. Rogers and McKim believe that Origen understood the purpose of the Bible was to lead persons to what they must know and believe

1. Jack Rogers, "The Church Doctrine of Biblical Authority," in *Biblical Authority*, ed. Jack Rogers (Waco, Tex.: Word, 1977), pp. 17–46.

in order to be saved. They say of his view, "Origen was completely conscious of the human character of the holy writings. He rejected any idea of a mechanical mode of inspiration, whether that of the prophets or of the biblical writers. He acknowledged that the New Testament evangelists and Paul expressed their own opinions, and that they could have erred while speaking on their own authority."[2]

This pattern is followed through the first part of the book. Reformation theology is to be understood in light of the strong emphasis on the Bible's saving function. Luther held much the same view of accommodation found earlier, but expressed it in light of the incarnation. Rogers and McKim say, "Luther's Christology strongly stressed the humanity of Christ. Similarly, he genuinely accepted fully the genuine humanity of Scripture. The mystery was not that God created some perfect and flawless form of words. The wonder was that God had chosen to use weak and imperfect human speech adequately to communicate his divine message."[3] The concept of error utilized by Luther must also be borne in mind: "When we read that statement ['There is no falsehood'] in context it is evident that Luther was not talking about factual errors or the lack of them. Luther was affirming the reliability of God's Word in accomplishing righteousness in the believer."[4]

The understanding of Calvin's view of Scripture proceeds along similar lines, but with some unique twists. Rogers and McKim stress Calvin's humanist training in literature and his law education, particularly as these affected his hermeneutics. They do not mention his well-known imagery of God as a nursemaid lisping to a child, but they nevertheless stress his accommodation of the truth to human recipients.[5] Further, they concentrate on Calvin the commentator. They contend that Calvin did not reject the idea of technical errors in writing. They say, "For Calvin, technical errors in the Bible that were the result of human slips of memory, limited knowledge, or the

2. Jack B. Rogers and Donald K. McKim, *The Authority and Interpretation of the Bible: An Historical Approach* (San Francisco: Harper and Row, 1979), p. 11.

3. Ibid., pp. 78–79.

4. Ibid., p. 88.

5. Ibid., pp. 98–100.

use of texts for different purposes than the original were all part of the normal human means of communication. They did not call into question the divine nature of Scripture's message. Nor did they hinder the completely adequate communication of God's Word."[6]

One thesis that runs throughout the historical part of the book is that a particular philosophical orientation makes a great deal of difference to one's view of Scripture. Rogers and McKim contrast Platonic with Aristotelian views. Platonism was rationalistic and deductive. It moved deductively from knowledge of the general principles to specific and concrete matters. In matters of theology, this led to a more fideistic stance. Aristotelianism, on the other hand, was empirical and inductive. It moved from the particular to the general. When applied to theology, this meant emphasizing reason as leading to faith.[7] Those who were basically Platonic in their philosophy, such as Augustine and Calvin, held to the authority of the Bible without requiring exact factual details, whereas those who were more Aristotelian insisted on the freedom of the Bible from any factual errors.

To recapitulate the argument to this point: Rogers and McKim contend that the view of complete factual inerrancy in all details was not really part of the historic orthodox position. Rather, that position could be better summarized as saying that the Bible is infallible in its message of salvation and things necessary to enable people to be saved. That, indeed, was the true Reformation position and thus the mainstream of Reformed theology. It was Protestant scholasticism that really originated the idea of inerrancy. As is well known, Protestant scholasticism spelled out doctrinal issues in greater detail than had been done previously. In the case of Lutheran scholasticism, for example, this involved great detail in the understanding of the incarnation, leading to such doctrines as the *communicatio idiomatum* (the idea that the qualities of Christ's deity are communicated to his humanity, and vice versa). It also led to rather extended speculation about the nature of biblical in-

6. Ibid., pp. 110–11.

7. Jack Rogers, "The Church Doctrine of Biblical Authority," in *Biblical Authority*, ed. Jack Rogers (Waco: Word, 1977), pp. 18–19.

spiration, so that some held that even the vowel points of the Old Testament Hebrew Masoretic text were inspired. On the Reformed side, it was Francis Turretin, who occupied the chair of theology at Geneva a century after Calvin, who really introduced the concept that Scripture must be fully inerrant in all matters, factual as well as theological. He followed the standard scholastic method that had been passed down by Aquinas and others, which involved a series of statements, objections, replies to objections, and the like. Whereas Calvin had rested belief in the divinity of Scripture on the internal witness of the Holy Spirit, Turretin based its divinity on its verbal inerrancy and rational proofs for that inerrancy. He was willing to rest the entire case for inerrancy on a single particular issue of truthfulness. He insisted that the prophets did not make mistakes in even the smallest particulars. If even a single error were to be found, that would call into question the entire issue of biblical inspiration and authority. How could something that was of divine origin possibly contain any error?[8]

Turretin used both external and internal evidences to prove the divine origin of the Bible. The external evidences are its antiquity, its duration, and the widespread agreement of many people. The internal evidences include its matter, its style, its form, and its effects. The success of the gospel and the conversion of the world proved the Bible's divinity.[9]

This commitment to the absolute inerrancy of the Bible meant that Turretin had to deal with all apparent discrepancies and flaws in it. He devoted a major portion of his *Institutio* to harmonizing twenty-three apparently conflicting passages. Rogers and McKim contend that whereas Calvin had thought of the Bible as written in human language God had utilized for his purpose, Turretin thought of the Bible's language as divinely dictated material. He did not utilize any concept of accommodation, such as Calvin and others had recourse to. And he even held that the inerrancy of the Bible extends to copies that we currently possess.[10]

8. Rogers and McKim, *Authority and Interpretation*, p. 176.
9. Ibid., p. 177.
10. Ibid.

It is when they come to the discussion of the "Old Princeton" School of biblical inspiration and authority that the argument advanced by Rogers and McKim becomes most pointed. They insist that the Westminster divines did not hold the modern view of inerrancy, emphasizing instead the internal witness of the Spirit and the idea that the primary purpose of Scripture is to bring persons to salvation.[11] It was not this view that was to become dominant, however. Protestant scholasticism gradually shifted the emphasis from Scripture's function to its form. A number of factors were at work. One was Newton's scientific theory, which emphasized the regularity of the universe. This, when applied to matters of religion and its implications drawn out, led to deism, which holds that God is the universal law giver but is not intimately involved with the system of nature. Locke's empirical philosophy was taken up by David Hume and extended, to the point that all we can possibly know are sense perceptions. There was consequent skepticism about anything going beyond that. In response to this, the Scottish clergyman and professor, Thomas Reid, developed what was to be known as Scottish commonsense philosophy or Scottish realism. He and one of his students, Dugald Stewart, believed that they were applying to philosophy the theory of Francis Bacon, which Newton had carried out in natural science. Rather than a deductive approach, Bacon had advocated an inductive approach, which would thus discover the fundamental principles and laws of the universe.[12]

Since both Reid and Stewart taught philosophy, they were aware of the problems presented by the philosophy of a fellow Scot, David Hume. Hume held that there is no way to be sure that the ideas in our minds actually correspond to external reality. This view, however, was unacceptable to Reid. Consequently, he modified the empirical philosophy by the addition of the concept of "judgment," an intuitive belief accompanying the perception of an object, that the object actually existed. The evidence of this judgment was "a strong and irresistible conviction and belief." This guaranteed the truth of sense perception

11. Ibid., pp. 207–9, 216–18.
12. Ibid., pp. 235–38.

and the validity of scientific induction. It was an appeal to the common sense, or common experience, of ordinary people.[13]

The transition to the American scene occurred with John Witherspoon, a Scottish minister, who came to the Colonies and became president of the College of New Jersey (later Princeton College) in 1768. He made Scottish realism the official philosophy of the college and each year delivered a series of lectures on moral philosophy to the seniors in Nassau Hall. In those lectures he influenced many future leaders of the Presbyterian Church and founders of Princeton Seminary. That institution came into being in 1812, largely through the leadership of Archibald Alexander, who was chosen by the General Assembly of the Church as the first president of the seminary. He had been tutored by William Graham, a graduate of Princeton College, who passed on verbatim to Alexander his notes from Witherspoon's lectures, thus introducing him to Scottish realism. Alexander required the theology students to read Turretin in Latin. In fact, Turretin was the text at Princeton until Charles Hodge wrote his systematic theology in 1872. Thus, the Old Princeton view of inspiration and inerrancy was a result of the blending of the scholastic theology of Turretin, the scientific views of Bacon, and the philosophy of Scottish common-sense realism. This meant that the teachings of the Bible and the findings of science must ultimately be in harmony with each other, and that the Bible must be fully truthful in all details of whatever subject it touched on.[14]

The basic thesis of the Rogers–McKim book thus emerges: the concept of inerrancy, as extending to factual details, was not part of the received orthodox tradition down through the years, including even the position of the Reformers. They, rather, held to the idea of accommodation of divine truth to human form, the emphasis on the saving purpose of the biblical revelation and the internal witness of the Spirit.[15] This strict concept of inerrancy resulted historically from blending the theology of Turretin and the philosophy of Scottish realism. Successively, under the teaching and writing of Charles

13. Ibid., pp. 239–41.
14. Ibid., pp. 265–310.
15. Ibid., pp. 98–106.

Hodge, a student and friend of Alexander, his son, A. A. Hodge, and B. B. Warfield, the Princeton view became widespread in the Presbyterian Church, as what Rogers and McKim consider to be modern Protestant scholasticism. Charles Hodge believed, in keeping with Scottish realism, that all humans follow certain universal patterns in their thinking. He had no idea that the Hebrews, for example, in their thinking, may have followed pictorial patterns rather than syllogistic logic.[16] This resulted in a particular understanding of the nature of meaning and of language. Rogers and McKim cite a well-known passage in Hodge's systematic theology about errors in the Bible being like a few grains of sand in the marble of the Parthenon. This admission of the existence of a few inconsequential errors in the Bible was by Hodge as a teacher; as a theorist, however, he maintained that all conflicts, both among different passages of the Bible and between the Bible and science, harmonized at all points. When pressed to reconcile the apparent conflicts of the Bible with the growing body of scientific data, he had recourse, late in life, to the distinction between the inerrant autographs and the existent copies, which may contain copyists' errors.[17]

As the tension between the Bible and science increased, A. A. Hodge and Warfield developed the theory of inspiration and inerrancy more fully and turned to a more apologetic task. Warfield believed that apologetics must be the very foundation on which systematic theology lies. Yet, when pressed by Henry Preserved Smith regarding details of scriptural phenomena, he made two significant moves. One was to restrict the doctrine of biblical inerrancy to the autographs of Scripture. The other was to rest the case for inerrancy on a doctrinal argument. This was the idea that the doctrine of inspiration, which he taught and which entailed the complete inerrancy of the Bible, was actually taught by Jesus and the apostles. He had done this through an argument establishing historically that this was the belief and teaching of the New Testament.[18]

16. Ibid., p. 284.
17. Ibid., p. 288.
18. Ibid., p. 344.

## The Inductive Approach to a Doctrine of Scripture

In the debate between Warfield and Smith, a difference of approach and method appeared that was to be very influential in years to come. Warfield maintained that the formulation of one's doctrine of Scripture was to be based on the Bible's didactic passages regarding its own nature. Smith's was based on the phenomenon of Scripture, that is, the actual nature of Scripture as the product of that process of inspiration.

This distinction became the grounds for the different view of inspiration propounded by some evangelicals in the last third of the twentieth century. One who particularly led the way was Dewey Beegle, at the time professor of Old Testament at Wesley Seminary in Washington, D.C. He emphasized the particulars of Scripture that appear to display discrepancies. His conclusion was that the Bible could not be considered inerrant, and that consequently, any theory of inspiration that implied such a conclusion must be rejected.[19]

Beegle calls attention to a number of passages that create problems for advocates of biblical inerrancy. Among them are the following:

1. Jude 14, where Jude writes, "It was of these also that Enoch in the seventh generation from Adam prophesied, saying," followed by a quotation from 1 Enoch 1:9. The specificity of his reference to "seventh from Adam," seems to indicate that he thought it was a statement from the historical character Enoch. Jude seems to have erred at this point.
2. Jude 9. Here Jude says, "But when the archangel Michael, contending with the devil, disputed about the body of Moses, he did not presume to pronounce a reviling judgment upon him, but said, 'The Lord rebuke you.'" This is not reported in any other canonical book. There was an early tradition, however, that the source was a portion of the apocryphal Assumption of Moses that was lost in the transmission. If this is the case,

however, then Jude simply incorporated the current tradition into his letter. But what then becomes of the doctrine of inerrancy?

3. The reign of Pekah, king of Israel, is said in 2 Kings 15:27 to have been twenty years, but this is now known to be incorrect, and efforts to resolve the problem have proven unsatisfactory.

4. The reign of Hezekiah, which is said in 2 Kings 18:1 to have begun in the third year of the reign of Hoshea (728) is now widely agreed by scholars to have been from 715 to 686. How is this discrepancy to be resolved?

5. Genesis 5. The genealogies here have traditionally been used to calculate a date for creation, anywhere from B.C. 3760 to B.C. 4004. Modern geology calls for much longer periods of time for the age of the earth. Efforts have been made to interpret these genealogies in less literal fashion, but it is apparent from the specificity of the references that they were intended literally.

6. Acts 7:4. In Stephen's speech, he says that Abraham left Haran after the death of his father Terah. Yet Genesis 11:26 says that Terah was 70 when Abraham was born and since he died in Haran at the age of 205 (11:32), Abraham was then 135. Since Genesis 12:4 says that Abraham left for Canaan when he was 75, that was 60 years before Terah's death, contradicting Acts 7:4.

7. Acts 7:15–16. Stephen says that Jacob was buried at Shechem in the tomb Abraham had bought from the sons of Hamor, whereas Genesis 50:13 indicates Hebron (Mamre). It was Joseph, according to Joshua 24:32, who was buried in the plot Jacob had purchased from the sons of Hamor.

8. In Galatians 3:16–17, Paul affirms that it was 430 years from the promise made to Abraham until the giving of the law. Yet, by combining the dates and ages in Genesis 12:4; 21:5; 25:26; and 47:9, we find that it was 215 years from the time Abraham went to Canaan until Jacob went to Egypt. This is in addition to the 430 years spent in Egypt (Exod. 12:40), giving a total of 645 years, rather than 430.

9. In Mark 14:30, 72, we are told that the cock crowed twice,

while the parallel accounts in Matthew (26:34, 74–75) and Luke (22:34, 60–61) mention only one occurrence.

10. First Corinthians 3:19 introduces a statement from Job 5:13 with the formula, "For it is written." Conservatives have usually equated this expression with "God says." Yet the source of the quotation is Eliphaz the Temanite, who has never been considered to have spoken under inspiration. While not an error as such, it does show a difference between the biblical data and a certain theory of inspiration.

11. There are also theological variations, or differences of interpretation of an event. A prime example is the case of David numbering Israel and Judah. According to 2 Samuel 24:1, the Lord incited David to do this, but 1 Chronicles 21:1 attributes this act to Satan's initiative.

On the basis of this kind of data, Beegle constructs his comprehensive view of Scripture and tradition. He states that "In all matters of faith and practice, therefore, Scripture is authentic, accurate, and trustworthy."[20] This sounds basically like the Fuller position of limited inerrancy. There is, however, a different twist to Beegle's view: "In a secondary, derivative fashion, therefore, the revelation and inspiration of God's Spirit continues. Accordingly, from the standpoint of *theological interpretation* the canon has never been closed. For this reason there is no basis in considering all of the biblical writers and editors as qualitatively different from postcanonical interpreters."[21] Another statement a page earlier sounds in some ways strangely like neoorthodoxy: "By the hearing, reading, and study of Scripture, revelation, inspiration, and authority become realities in every earnest heart through the agency of the same Spirit who watched over Scripture's recording and transmission."[22] This hypothesis is lent support by his approving citation later of Emil Brunner in agreement with his distinction between objective and subjective truth.[23]

20. Ibid., p. 308.
21. Ibid.
22. Ibid., p. 307.
23. Ibid., p. 310.

Beegle himself was not active in evangelical circles, but his arguments enunciated in print what a number of evangelical scholars, especially in the biblical fields, had been saying. As such, they are a good representation of some of the newer evangelical objections to the idea of strict biblical inerrancy.

## Biblical Criticism

The other major issue that came out of the Warfield–Smith debate was the legitimacy and extent of the role to be played by biblical criticism. This is another area that has become very significant in current evangelical debate about the doctrine of Scripture. The study and use of biblical criticism have moved through several significant stages. Textual criticism is the study of the various versions of a given passage, which tries to determine as closely as possible the correct reading of the original text. Because of the high value conservative Christians place on the biblical text, determining its exact, correct reading is very important to them; consequently, evangelical biblical scholars have been leaders in the practice of this area of criticism. Source criticism is the endeavor to determine the written sources from which the original writing was composed or derived. Form criticism is the study of the prewritten stage of the tradition, to determine the oral traditions that may have shaped it. Here the conception is that the community of the church, as it passed on and proclaimed the tradition, selected and shaped it. Finally, for our purposes, is redaction criticism. This is a study of the way in which the author of a given Gospel, for example, modified the tradition that he received, interpreting it in terms of his own purpose in writing.

As noted, there was considerable opposition to the use of any form of biblical criticism other than textual criticism by the Princeton theology, especially in its latter stages. Because historical criticism was used by liberal theologians and formed the basis of much of their argumentation of the conservative view, it was not believed to be a legitimate tool for use by conservatives. Gradually, however, conservatives began to make use of some of these methods in a limited fashion. This has been especially true of the use of redaction criticism by evangelical Gospels scholars. There are, of course, various conceptions of what activity the Gospel writer might have engaged in. Some would say that such activity was restricted to selection of material, or perhaps to emphasis of certain material, or possibly to the paraphrase of some of Jesus' sayings, for example. Or, some would say that there may have been reordering of material, rearranging of the things that were said on a topical, rather than a chronological, basis. Such activities, evangelicals have often said, are not inconsistent with the doctrine of biblical inerrancy.

When, however, a Gospel writer is said to have created words and placed them in the mouth of Jesus, or to have altered the tradition, transforming one account into another similar but different one, difficulty has arisen within evangelical circles. While a number of Gospels specialists in evangelical schools were apparently teaching such a view, they were, for the most part, not publishing their theories, and so they were attracting relatively little attention. One example that did appear in print was Robert Guelich's reworked dissertation on the Sermon on the Mount, but relatively little notice was taken of it.[24] It was Robert Gundry's commentary on Matthew that was to herald the presence of new views among evangelicals, and also to provoke a strong reaction from more conservative evangelicals.

Gundry had previously produced some publications that took a clearly conservative stand, such as *The Use of the Old Testament in Saint Matthew's Gospel; With Special Reference to the Messianic Hope.*[25] In this commentary, however, his view apparently developed as he proceeded through the Book of Matthew, as he indicates in his preface. He notes that his comments on the nativity passages "had to be completely rewritten once I saw how freely and creatively Matthew edited his sources in the rest of his gospel."[26]

24. Robert A. Guelich, *The Sermon on the Mount: A Foundation for Understanding* (Waco, Tex.: Word, 1982).

25. Robert H. Gundry, *The Use of the Old Testament in Saint Matthew's Gospel; With Special Reference to the Messianic Hope* (Leiden: Brill, 1967).

26. Robert H. Gundry, *Matthew: A Commentary on His Literary and Theological Art* (Grand Rapids: Eerdmans, 1982), p. xi.

In Gundry's comments on these passages we see a picture of
Matthew clearly modifying the material he received from Luke.
So, for example, Gundry says of the annunciation to Joseph:
"Matthew turns the annunciation to Mary before her conceiv-
ing Jesus (Luke 1:26–38) into an annunciation to Joseph after
her conceiving Jesus."[27] Gundry sees a similar modification by
Matthew in connection with the account of the visit of the
Magi: "Matthew now turns the visit of the local Jewish shep-
herds (Luke 2:8–20) into the adoration by Gentile magi from
foreign parts."[28]

What is most instructive about the problems faced by evangelical biblical critics is the nature of the explanation of the
specific content of Matthew's Gospel. It is accounted for en-
tirely on the basis of Matthew's intentions and actions. The
possibility of a special revelation to Matthew, apart from the
material in Luke that he utilized, is not really considered. It is
often said that biblical criticism in itself is not bad, that the
method must be evaluated in terms of the presuppositions that
underlie it. In general, if these are naturalistic, they are considered inappropriate, as thus prejudging the possibility of a revelation that claims historical actions of a supernatural being
that are discontinuous with natural laws. Such naturalistic or
anti-supernaturalistic presuppositions may be present and
functioning at three different levels, however:

1. Primary naturalism. The causation of the events reported in Scripture must be explained on natural
   grounds.
2. Secondary naturalism. The writing of the Scriptures
   and the inclusion and interpretation of certain materials must be explained on natural grounds.
3. Tertiary naturalism. The interpretation of the Scriptures is done by the use of natural human methods of
   interpretation of literature, with no special illuminat-
   ing work attributed to the Holy Spirit.

27. Ibid., p. 20.
28. Ibid., p. 26.

This approach practiced by Gundry would appear to be a case of secondary naturalism. The real issue here, as well as in other evangelicals' use of critical methodology, is whether revelation to the writer of material not in the tradition is a possibility.

## The Conflict of Revelational and Traditional Ideas

One of the ideas that liberal theologians sometimes advanced was the idea that Scripture contains the Word of God, that is, that some parts of it are revealed and other parts are simply reflections of general cultural understandings. The task then becomes one of sifting through the material and determining which is which. Generally, evangelical theologians had not accepted or endorsed such a view.

In 1975, however, a book appeared that seemed to present a theory considerably like this. The book, *Man as Male and Female*, was written by Paul K. Jewett, professor of systematic theology at Fuller Seminary. It was an attempt to grapple with Paul's sometimes contrasting statements on the role of women in society, the family, and the church. Jewett acknowledges Paul's background as a rabbi and the view of women that he would have been taught and accepted. This was one of clear subordination, even inferiority, of women to men. On the other hand, Jesus had elevated the status of women, never dominating them or treating them as inferiors. These two influences, the old and the new, were operative in Paul's life and thought. Jewett describes this contrast: "So far as he thought in terms of his Jewish background, he thought of the woman as subordinate to the man for whose sake she was created (1 Cor. 11:9). But so far as he thought in terms of the new insight he had gained through the revelation of God in Christ, he thought of the woman as equal to the man in all things, the two having been made one in Christ, in whom there is neither male nor female (Gal. 3:28)."[29]

Jewett elaborates and explains this basic contrast. He says that "there is no satisfying way to harmonize the Pauline argument for female subordination with the larger Christian vision

29. Paul K. Jewett, *Man as Male and Female: A Study of Sexual Relationships from a Theological Point of View* (Grand Rapids: Eerdmans, 1975), p. 112.

of which the great apostle to the Gentiles was himself the primary architect."[30] Jewett believes that Paul was aware that the view of women that he had inherited from his Jewish rabbinic background was somewhat incongruous with his new insights and that he was somewhat uncomfortable with this tension. Jewett rejects some of the traditional means of harmonization, such as the idea that Paul's statement about women in the church being silent was referring, not to all women at all times, but only to those women who were disturbing worship services in Corinth.[31]

Jewett contends that Paul always based his arguments on the second creation account (Gen. 2:18–23), never the first. Furthermore, Paul's interpretation of that passage is based on the traditional rabbinic interpretation, that the order of the creation supports the idea of the superiority of man over woman. Jewett then poses the crucial question: "Is this rabbinic interpretation of Gen. 2:18f. correct? We do not think that it is, for it is palpably inconsistent with the first creation narrative, with the life style of Jesus, and with the apostle's own clear affirmation that in Christ there is no male or female (Gal. 3:28)."[32]

This problem of interpretation shows itself in other areas of Paul's thought. So, for example, the apostle's injunction to slaves to obey their masters, in the Ephesian *Haustafel*, "surely reflects the historical limitations of his Christian thought."[33] Jewett then goes on to apply this method of interpretation to another item in the list. "Now if the apostle's ambivalent view of the slave/master relationship reflects the historical limitations out of which he wrote the Ephesian *Haustafel*, then the same may be said of his view of the male/female relationship whereby women as such, by the Creator's intent, are subordinate to men."[34]

This represented, even by Fuller Seminary standards, a somewhat novel and radical approach. It smacked of some of the hermeneutical methods of more liberal scholars, such as W. D. Davies, who contends that Paul changed his view of the

30. Ibid., pp. 112–13.
31. Ibid., p. 115.
32. Ibid., p. 119.
33. Ibid., p. 138.
34. Ibid., p. 139.

resurrection of believers between the writing of 1 Corinthians 15 and 2 Corinthians 5.[35] A committee was appointed to investigate Jewett's views, and a majority concluded that Jewett was wrong in his interpretation of Paul. They also indicated that they believed that Jewett was sincere in his subscription to the school's affirmation that the Bible is the only infallible rule of faith and practice.[36]

## The Influence of Barth

We noted in the chapter on methodology an increased openness toward the theology of Karl Barth. Such an influence, by its very nature, appears most clearly in the doctrine of Scripture. Although there have been few direct acknowledgments of the influence of Barth, there are nonetheless echoes of a nonpropositional or personal view of revelation.

One of the most explicit is that of Bernard Ramm. Ramm argues that Barth has been misunderstood, and that his actual views are closer to the traditional evangelical position than many have thought. He describes what he calls the idea of diastasis between revelation and the Bible in Barth's theology. Rather than an inerrant and infallible original text, Barth pushes the matter back another step. God is infallible, not any human document. This involves some initial distinction between the Word of God and the Bible: "The primal meaning of the Word of God is God in his self-disclosure; God in his act of revelation, which is (as it originates in God) infallible, inerrant, and indefectible."[37] The attempt of some evangelicals to insist on every word being exactly what God intended and therefore inerrant, is based on a misunderstanding of the nature of language. The concepts of the indirect identity of the Word of God and Holy Scripture and of the brokenness or defraction of revelation, as well as the idea that Scripture is a witness to revelation, are Barth's expressions of the diastasis. Ramm maintains

35. W. D. Davies, *Paul and Rabbinic Judaism: Some Rabbinic Elements in Pauline Theology* (London: SPCK, 1955), chapter 10.

36. George M. Marsden, *Reforming Fundamentalism: Fuller Seminary and the New Evangelicalism* (Grand Rapids: Eerdmans, 1975), pp. 280–82.

37. Bernard Ramm, *After Fundamentalism: The Future of Evangelical Theology* (San Francisco: Harper and Row, 1983), p. 90.

that in practice many evangelicals do this as well, when they separate cultural matters from pure timeless revelation or emphasize the humanness of Scripture. Barth's virtue is that he does this self-consciously and explicitly. Ramm argues that for Barth there is objective content to the revelation, as expressed in the idea that the Word of God is in the text as *Bild*, or picture, the idea of *Sache*, or substance or meaning of a piece of literature, and the concept of the *Wort* (word) in the words.[38]

It is apparent that Ramm has changed his interpretation of Barth from an earlier position.[39] We could debate the extent to which this later interpretation of Barth is correct. It is apparent, however, that a shift toward a more ambiguous relationship between revelation and the words of Scripture has taken place in Ramm's view of Scripture.

Another individual who made rather explicit acknowledgment of a change of his own view is George Ladd. In an article in *Interpretation* in 1971, he stated that he "cannot assent to the older orthodox view . . . that 'revelation, in the biblical sense of the term, is the communication of information.'" Rather, he says, his view is now that "revelation moves in the dimension of personal encounter. . . . God reveals *himself.*" He does indicate that his view is that "what God reveals is not only information about himself; he reveals *himself*" and agrees with James Barr that sometimes God reveals himself by words alone.[40] It appears that he has not abandoned the idea of propositional or informational revelation, but is more open than some earlier orthodox theologians to the personal revelation taught by Barth.

Pinnock, in his latest writings, also indicates greater openness to personal revelation. In *The Scripture Principle* he rejects the argument made by Rogers and McKim, that strict inerrancy is a late departure from historic orthodoxy. He believes John Woodbridge's critique is basically effective, and that orthodoxy has neglected the idea of the humanity of the Bible.[41]

---

38. Ibid., pp. 92–94.

39. Bernard Ramm, *The Pattern of Religious Authority* (Grand Rapids: Eerdmans, 1959), pp. 97–98.

40. George E. Ladd, "The Search for Perspective," *Interpretation* 25.1 (January 1971): 62.

41. Clark Pinnock, *The Scripture Principle* (San Francisco: Harper and Row, 1984), p. xii.

He definitely speaks of the Bible as "a deposit of propositional truth,"[42] but is concerned that both the objective and subjective aspects of revelation be maintained. In particular, he wants to maintain the emphasis on the internal working of the Holy Spirit in conjunction with the objective word of Scripture. At times this sounds simply like the traditional doctrine of illumination: "He [the Spirit] helps us to receive it as the Word of God and to understand what it means for our time."[43] What is interesting about Pinnock's view, however, is the idea that revelation is not limited to the original giving of the Scriptures or to the original intent of the text: "The possibilities of meaning are not limited to the original intent of the text, although that is the anchor of interpretation, but can arise from the interaction of the Spirit and the Word."[44] Again, he seems to extend genuine revelation beyond Scripture: "Revelation has not ceased. A phase of it has ceased, the phase that provided the gospel and its scriptural witness, but not revelation in every sense. . . . Indeed, indications are that the Spirit continues to address us through one another, through gifts like prophecy, for example." He then goes on to liken our situation to that in the New Testament church: "We ought not to despise prophecy just because we rightly fear false prophecy. The secret is to be critical of prophetic claims and discern what is authentic (1 Thess. 5:19–22). . . . The point is simply that we ought not to suppress the Spirit in his revealing work but to be docile and receptive in his presence."[45]

One does not want to be unfair to Pinnock here, for it is apparent that his aim is not to propound a Barthian view of revelation but to revitalize the evangelical doctrine of illumination of Scripture by the Holy Spirit. Yet, at some points, he clearly goes beyond the traditional form of that doctrine, insisting that what the Holy Spirit speaks today is not limited to the original intent of the text, and that revelation may come to us, not merely through the Bible, but through contemporary prophets as well.

42. Ibid., p. 18.
43. Ibid., p. 163.
44. Ibid.
45. Ibid.

Donald Bloesch is an evangelical who fits this part of the movement in many ways. Certainly, in his strong stand against a certain kind of feminism in the church, he does not participate in the general mood of the postconservative evangelicals.[46] His view of Scripture places him more correctly within this stream of religious life and theology, however. He also insists on the full authority of the Bible, but is leery of fundamentalism's approach, both in its insistence on total accuracy in all details referred to and in the use of rational evidences in support of the view of the Bible.[47] He suggests that there have been three basic approaches to Scripture in the history of the church. The first, the sacramental, sees "revelation essentially as God in action and Scripture as the primary channel or medium of revelation."[48] Here he places Augustine, Calvin, Luther, Edwards, Bavinck, Kuyper, Geoffrey Bromiley, and G. C. Berkouwer. The second approach, the scholastic, "understands revelation as the disclosure of a higher truth that nonetheless stands in continuity with rational or natural truth. The Bible becomes a book of revealed propositions which are directly accessible to reason and which contains no errors in any respect."[49] Here he lists not only the Protestant scholastics such as Turretin and Warfield, but also contemporaries such as Gordon Clark, Francis Schaeffer, Carl Henry, and John Warwick Montgomery. The third is the liberal-modernist approach, which sees revelation as "inner enlightenment or self discovery," with the Bible then being a record of such experiences. He lists here such persons as Schleiermacher, Troeltsch, Fosdick, John A. T. Robinson, and Rudolf Bultmann.[50]

Bloesch chooses to identify with the sacramental approach. He appreciates the task that Barth has done in restoring this approach, although he is not uncritical of Barth. He insists, however, that the sacramental approach does not rule out cognitive revelation. The revelation is not simply *through* Scrip-

---

46. Donald G. Bloesch, *The Battle for the Trinity: The Debate over Inclusive God-Language* (Ann Arbor, Mich.: Vine Books, Servant Publications, 1985).

47. Donald G. Bloesch, *Essentials of Evangelical Theology*, vol. 2, *Life, Ministry, and Hope* (San Francisco: Harper and Row, 1978), pp. 267, 270.

48. Ibid., p. 270.

49. Ibid.

50. Ibid., pp. 270–71.

ture, but *as* Scripture. "Yet this is not to say that the words of Scripture are directly revealed (as in the scholastic approach) but that Scripture embodies the truth that God wants us to hear. The unity between the revealed word, Jesus Christ, and the written word lies both in the inspiration of the Scripture, whereby he guarantees a trustworthy witness to Christ, and in his revelatory action, in which he speaks through this witness to people of every age (cf. 1 Cor. 2:10–13)."[51]

While this role of the Bible is functional, it is not simply functional. When we say that the Bible is the Word of God, we mean two things by this: "that all the words are selected by the Spirit of God through his guidance of the human authors; and that the truth of God is enshrined in and mediated through these words."[52] The use together of two terms, "enshrined in" and "mediated through," suggests a somewhat dialectical relationship of revelation and the Bible, as Bloesch indicates further: "The Bible is neither the direct, unmediated speech of God (as we sometimes find in Warfield) nor simply an indirect historical witness to divine revelation (as in Barth). It is the Word of God in human clothing, the revelation of God transmitted through human concepts and imagery."[53] It appears that we have here a view of revelation and the Bible that is basically the orthodox view, but influenced by elements of Barth's view.

Finally, we have the revisioned view of biblical authority proposed by Stanley Grenz. He is critical of the typical evangelical approach to authority, which proceeds from revelation, inspiration, biblical authority, and illumination.[54] He is quite definite about his rejection of this approach: "we can no longer construct our doctrine of Scripture in the classical manner. The assertion of the inspiration of Scripture cannot function as the theological premise from which bibliology emerges, nor as the focal point of our understanding of the relation between the Spirit and Scripture." He suggests instead a closer connection between inspiration and illumination.[55] In this he seems to be

51. Ibid., pp. 271–72.
52. Ibid., pp. 272–73.
53. Ibid., p. 273.
54. Stanley J. Grenz, *Revisioning Evangelical Theology: A Fresh Agenda for the 21st Century* (Downers Grove, Ill.: InterVarsity, 1993), p. 116.
55. Ibid., p. 118.

criticizing even Clark Pinnock's approach to illumination. So Grenz includes his discussion of the doctrine of Scripture under the doctrine of the Holy Spirit, two-thirds of the way through his systematic theology.

Grenz asserts that the confession of the inspiration of Scripture arose within the community as the church experienced the power and spirit of the truth of God through these Scriptures. Unlike the usual evangelical view of inspiration that thinks of the production of the writings on the model of single authorship, Grenz sees a close tie between the community and the production of Scripture. While inspiration includes the writing of books by individual authors, it also involves the community, including oral traditions and other source materials. So "the writings contained in the Bible represent the self-understanding of the community in which it developed."[56] Like Ramm, Grenz declares that one who "pioneered a revisioned doctrine of Scripture was Karl Barth." He observes that "for Barth the revelatory nature of the Bible is dependent on its function as a witness to the revelation of God in Jesus." While asserting that as evangelicals "we may rightly resist what we find to be Barth's inordinate emphasis on the character event of revelation, he is surely correct in this delineation of the relationship between Scripture and Christ."[57] Grenz links this both to his understanding of narrative and of the community: "The Scriptures provide the categories by which we can understand ourselves and organize our narratives."[58]

## Evaluation

We have examined a collage of views making up the postconservative understanding of Scripture. While differing in some ways and in some emphases, they all nonetheless show some changes from the evangelicalism of the previous generation. Thus, some of the positive comments as well as some of the negative criticisms will apply more to some varieties than to others, while some observations are applicable to all.

56. Ibid., p. 121.
57. Ibid., p. 129.
58. Ibid., p. 136.

## Positive

1. These theologians have rightly reminded us that theologies are shaped and expressed within particular historical and cultural situations. Some of the emphases in a given theology must therefore be understood in light of the situations from which they stemmed and the issues they were addressing.
2. They have correctly pointed out the sometimes one-sidedness of the evangelical understanding of the nature of Scripture, in stressing its divine aspect to the neglect of the human.
3. They have also pointed out the sometimes onesided nature of the evangelical understanding of authority. Unlike the Reformation principle of the union of Word and Spirit, fundamentalists have sometimes so strongly emphasized the objective dimensions, the fact that the Bible is objectively the Word of God, that it has become a formal principle. To read the Bible was to have truth in one's possession. These men have reminded us of the importance of illumination and application of the Word by the Spirit.
4. By the renewed emphasis on illumination by the Spirit, these theologians have given the Bible back to the Christian laity. Sometimes, the impression has been conveyed that the Bible can only be understood and interpreted by technical exegetes. While not neglecting the dimension of scholarly exegesis, these postconservatives have stressed that since the Holy Spirit dwells in all believers, he is also able to give understanding through illumination.
5. These theologians have correctly pointed out the earthly character of the biblical writings. These have not simply been dropped directly from heaven. They bear the marks of the persons and the cultures to which they came.
6. These theologians have rightly reminded us of the variety of literary materials and modalities of revelation found in the Bible. Revelation did not simply come in revealed propositions in the primary sense, in every case. Revelation as God's divine act is a very real matter.

### Negative

1. The historical analysis presented by Rogers and McKim has the appearance of a very scholarly piece of work, with many footnotes. Historian John Woodbridge, however, subjected the book to a devastating criticism. He showed that its thesis was supported by very careful selection of materials and the use of secondary sources in many cases. When seen in a light of fuller examination of church history and a more careful use of historical method, their thesis is at variance with the facts.[59] Although occasionally misunderstanding their statements,[60] his argument was very well documented and the conclusions sound. Even Pinnock acknowledges this, as indicated above.

2. One of the points made most consistently by postconservatives is their rejection of objective proofs for the inspiration and authority of the Bible, and of a Bible that must give inerrant history. The conviction of the Bible's divine origin originates instead in a personal experience, effected by the Holy Spirit. The evidence, therefore, is subjective rather than objective. This argument, however, seems to proceed within a basically Christian context. We now are aware of the claims of other religions, whose adherents are to be found even within what have previously been primarily Christian cultures. Many of them have the same sort of subjective certitude about the validity of their faith as do Christians. If indeed postconservative evangelicals hold that Christianity is the true religion, they must make some note of this phenomenon and offer a further reason for their conclusion. If not, this either looks like ethnocentrism or at least ignorance of the postmodern scene.

3. There is also a rather serious epistemological problem, especially with the idea of limited inerrancy. This view contends that the Bible is not necessarily accurate in its

59. John D. Woodbridge, *Biblical Authority: A Critique of the Rogers–McKim Proposal* (Grand Rapids: Zondervan, 1982).

60. Cf. his reversal of the inductive–deductive paradigm with respect to Plato and Aristotle, ibid., p. 79.

historical and scientific statements, in other words, those references that can be checked empirically. It is, however, to be considered infallible or inerrant in its theological or religious or revealed statements. The difficulty comes not with the rejection of the idea of inerrancy or infallibility of the former, but in the attribution of infallibility to the latter. The difficulty is not that these theologians believe too little, but that they believe too much. If the Bible is not necessarily accurate in those areas in which we can check it, on what possible grounds is it considered infallible where we can? Without some support for this ad hoc hypothesis, this seems to revert back to the difficulties noted in criticism 2 above.

4. There is a lack of clarity about the relationship of propositions of theology to revelation that is not always considered propositional. This is the same criticism frequently raised against the view of Karl Barth, and to the extent that these theologians reflect a similar view, they are also vulnerable to that criticism. As noted in our discussion of Bloesch's view, there is a somewhat dialectical relationship between revelation and the Bible.

5. For the most part, there is an "inductive" approach to settling the question of the Bible's inerrancy, as we saw most clearly in the examination of Beegle's view. Actually the contrasting view is also based on an induction, but an induction of different data, namely, biblical teaching. A more accurate designation, therefore, would be to say that this is an approach that emphasizes the phenomena of the Bible, or the results of revelation and inspiration, rather than the biblical teaching about these topics. Note, however, that this means following a different methodology here than what these theologians (with the possible exception of Grenz) would follow with respect to the other loci of theology. There, the doctrine of sanctification or the doctrine of the church is generally based on the didactic passages about those topics, rather than narrative passages that illustrate the results of God's work in those areas. This introduces an inconsistency

in the method. In Grenz's case, since the object of theology is the community of faith's reflection on its own
faith, it may be that the method of the doctrine of
Scripture is being consistently applied to the other
areas of doctrine.

6. There is, particularly in Grenz's view, no distinction
between the source and the norm of theology; the
terms are, in fact, used interchangeably. This, however, seems to confuse two types of authority, or two
roles of authorities, of originating or supplying the
content of a theology and of interpreting, evaluating,
or judging such content. This is the distinction I have
referred to elsewhere as the legislative and the judicial
authorities.[61]

We have seen that in a number of ways some evangelicals
were beginning to modify the traditional evangelical view of
the doctrine of Scripture early in the second half of the twentieth century. At the time, some contended that a doctrine like
biblical inerrancy was a peripheral matter, and ridiculed any
sort of "domino theory" that suggested that modification of
other doctrines would result. As we shall see in the succeeding
chapters, however, changes have begun to appear in other doctrines as well.

61. Millard J. Erickson, *Christian Theology* (Grand Rapids: Baker, 1986), p.
257.

# 4 The Doctrine of God

**The** doctrine of God has become the focus of more intense attention in recent years on the part of postconservative evangelical theologians than virtually any other doctrine. In large part they express a sense that the traditional (or "classical") view of God is no longer adequate. Consequently, to understand this view of God it is necessary first to examine the major features of the more traditional view, and then to observe those developments that have called it into question.

## The Classical View of God

The orthodox conception of God was one of the first doctrines to be worked out and is basic to the whole theological system. The Apostles' Creed begins with the words, "I believe in God the Father Almighty, maker of heaven and earth." This terminology captures the basic nature of God—he is a perfect, complete, and infinite being. He is perfect in all of his characteristics, or attributes, as theologians have generally referred to them. So, for example, he is all-powerful, able to do all things. He is all-knowing, aware of and understanding all truth. He is eternal, without beginning or end. He is omnipresent, active everywhere within the creation. He is independent of the creation, not needing it, but having brought it into existence by his will and action. He is free, not compelled by anything other than his own nature. He is completely good morally and spiritually. There is no lack of any kind in him.

As this understanding was worked out, it became subject to more specific, refined interpretations. So, for example, the concept of impassibility was developed. This was subject to a number of variations, but basically meant the independence of God. He is not affected by anything. The tranquillity of his emotions is not disturbed by anything humans do. In some forms, especially the Thomistic variety that drew heavily on the thought of Aristotle, this came to mean a God who was aloof and unmoved by the condition of humans. The eternity of God also came to be understood not as unending time, but as timelessness, as God existed not within time but outside it. God's omniscience was complete, including foreknowledge, or complete knowledge of the future, including the actions of humans. While not all who held the orthodox view subscribed to all of the details of Thomism, it was Thomism that came to be thought of as the classical doctrine.

A number of factors arose to challenge this orthodox synthesis. Part of it was simply the twentieth-century hostility toward any sort of metaphysics. Since the time of Immanuel Kant, there had been skepticism regarding the possibility of theoretical knowledge of supersensible objects. The trend became most pronounced, however, in the form of logical positivism, which claimed that any synthetic statements (that is, statements in which the predicate purports to add something not implicit in the subject) that could not show the sense data that would verify or falsify them, were meaningless. If accepted, this meant that the traditional theological statements had to be understood as either expressions of the feelings or consciousness of the person, or as ethical statements, such as intentions to act in a particular way. Philosophy, in most secular institutions, became an analysis of language, rather than making any sort of normative statements about the nature of things.

## The Process View of God

This trend naturally constituted a severe threat to orthodox Christian theology, with its emphasis on an existent God, a strongly metaphysical conception. Into this situation came a proposed solution known as process theology which, however, actually posed an additional problem for the classical view. It accepted many of the conclusions of modern learning, and sought to construct its picture of reality, and ultimately its understanding of God, on them. One of these was the revised view of reality posed by twentieth-century physics. Newtonian physics had understood reality as composed of substances, fixed entities possessing definite characteristics. While it could change (or exchange) these attributes, the substance was the remaining factor, the point of identity. Permanent qualities were thought to be the norm, and it was change and motion that needed to be explained.

Einsteinian physics understood reality more dynamically and more relatively, however. And process philosophy built on the idea of change, rather than permanence, as the key to its philosophy. Rather than substances as the basic building blocks of reality, this philosophy considered the event to be the key. All reality was pictured as events or occurrences, each of which has two poles. The event prehends, or grasps, other events or actual occasions. This is its physical pole. It also prehends the eternal objects, which are forms, qualities, relations, abstracted from any concrete instances of them. This is its mental pole. God is the one who gives to each actual occasion its initial aim, some purpose that he has for it. Each such occasion can then choose its subjective aim, what it seeks to realize, which may or may not be the initial aim God has supplied it.[1]

What is interesting for our purposes is that in this scheme of things God so participates in the whole web of reality that he, too, has a bipolar nature. He has both an abstract essence and a concrete actuality. In the former respect, he is eternal, absolute, independent, and unchangeable. Such abstract attributes as omniscience are to be found here. With respect to the concrete actuality, however, God is contingent, dependent, temporal, relative, and constantly changing. His knowledge is a consequent knowledge, that is, his knowledge is dependent on the decisions and actions of individuals within the world. Whereas classical orthodoxy thought of God as having only the one pole, that of the eternal and absolute, process theology understands him to have both poles. This is an indication of how immanent within the process God is thought to be, that he participates in the same categories as the rest of reality.[2]

1. John B. Cobb Jr., *A Christian Natural Theology; Based on the Thought of Alfred North Whitehead* (Philadelphia: Westminster, 1965), pp. 30–39.

2. Ibid., pp. 161–64.

The contrast with the orthodox understanding of God is seen clearly in the statement by David Griffin and John Cobb of the views of God or aspects of the doctrine that they reject.[3]

1.  God as cosmic moralist. This concept may take varying forms, any of which is unacceptable to the process theist. The worst variety of this conception is the picture of God as a divine lawgiver and judge, who has set forth an arbitrarily defined collection of moral rules, keeps record of human beings' conformity or nonconformity to these rules, and rewards and punishes people accordingly. A more enlightened version is a god whose most fundamental concern is the fostering of moral attitudes.

2.  God as unchanging and passionless absolute. This concept of God as completely unchanging, unaffected by anything external to himself and without any passion or emotion, derives from Greek thought. It has, however, played a prominent part in much classical theology. On this conception, the world is totally dependent on God and wholly external to him. Yet he is completely independent of it, utterly unaffected by anything that occurs in it.

3.  God as controlling power. This is the idea that God is in absolute control of the world, determining every detail of what occurs in it; for example, God takes the life of a person who dies, or spares someone from danger. Process theology, however, asks what kind of a God favors one person over another in dispensing the circumstances of life.

4.  God as sanctioner of the status quo. This is the idea that God is primarily interested in order. If God is the controlling power, then what is, is because he has brought it about. Therefore, obedience to God requires preserving the status quo.

5.  God as male. Not only are the members of the Trinity regarded as male, but God is seen as totally independent, powerful, and unresponsive. This dominant, in-

3. John B. Cobb and David Ray Griffin, *Process Theology: An Introductory Exposition* (Philadelphia: Westminster, 1976), pp. 8–10.

flexible, unemotional God is the archetype of the "strong" male.

Of each of these views, Cobb and Griffin say, "Process theology denies the existence of this God." Whether all these qualities inhere in the orthodox understanding of God, it is clear that at least some of them do. There is therefore clearly a conflict between process theology's view of God and traditional or orthodox theology's view.

## The Open View of God

For the most part, postconservatives have taken pains to distinguish their view from process theology. One evangelical who openly acknowledges his acceptance of process thought is Gregory Boyd, who states that "the fundamental vision of the process world view, especially as espoused by Charles Hartshorne, is correct," and attempts to construct an interpretation of the Trinity by making some modifications of process thought.[4] Another is Stephen Franklin, who found in Whitehead's thought "a profound metaphysical vision which allowed for the possibility of God-language conveying genuine claims about what is the case."[5] Richard Rice indicates certain points of commonality between free will theism and process thought. He says, "The concept of God proposed here shares the process view that God's relation to the temporal world consists in a succession of concrete experiences, rather than a single timeless perception." More important is his next statement: "It also shares with process theism the twofold analysis of God, or the 'dipolar theism,' described above. It conceives God as both absolute and relative, necessary and contingent, eternal and temporal, changeless and changing. It attributes one element in each pair of contrasts to the appropriate aspect of God's being—the essential divine character or

4. Gregory A. Boyd, *Trinity and Process: A Critical Evaluation and Reconstruction of Hartshorne's Di-polar Theism Towards a Trinitarian Metaphysics* (New York: Peter Lang, 1992), preface.

5. Stephen T. Franklin, *Speaking from the Depths: Alfred North Whitehead's Hermeneutical Metaphysics of Propositions, Experience, Symbolism, Language, and Religion* (Grand Rapids: Eerdmans, 1990), p. ix.

the concrete divine experience."[6] He goes on to point out that there are significant differences between the two, but this certainly sounds like the acknowledgment of the presence of at least some process categories. Clark Pinnock, in his chapter on process thought, criticizes both process theology and the classical theistic view, identifying his position as somewhere midway between the two views.[7] He contends that the major point of distinction is that the open view does not consider God dependent on the creation, as process theology does.[8]

At points in the exposition of the open view of God we will see items of similarity to process theology. It will remain for the reader to judge the extent of dependence of the one on the other.

*Human freedom.* One crucial point in the argument of free will theism is, as its self-designated name would indicate, the emphasis on human freedom. This has been an increasing thrust of much twentieth-century thought, but especially of existentialism. Existentialists have insisted on radical human freedom, as contrasted with any kind of determinism. Indeed, excusing oneself on the basis of any sort of determinism, whether genetic or social, is invalid, and is a case of what Martin Heidegger termed "inauthenticity." The existentialist treatment of freedom is both descriptive and prescriptive. Humans are declared to be free, but beyond that they are urged to choose freely, rather than going along with conventional opinion or conforming to pressures of the crowd. In a sense, existentialists never really argued for this view of freedom. It is simply a presupposition, an unquestioned starting point in light of which all of thought and life must be constructed. Jean-Paul Sartre's atheism is well known. What is less widely known and understood, however, is the basis for the atheism. There cannot be a god, for if there were, he would be a major encroachment on my freedom. I know, however, that I am free. Therefore, there is no God.

6. Richard Rice, *God's Foreknowledge and Man's Free Will* (Minneapolis: Bethany, 1985), p. 33.

7. Clark H. Pinnock, "Between Classical and Process Theism," in *Process Theology,* ed. Ronald Nash (Grand Rapids: Baker, 1987), pp. 313–14.

8. Ibid., pp. 318–20.

As we proceed through the discussion of the open view of God, we shall see that this same assumption of human freedom lies at the center of much of the discussion. Not only the control of human behavior, but even the knowledge of future human actions would militate against humans being truly free. Consequently, those doctrines, as held in classical theism, must be modified.

The free will theists see their view as quite different from the classical view in many ways. They see the latter view as being that of an absolute, perfect God, who is outside of time, knows everything, and controls or causes all that occurs. Further, he is something of an aloof monarch. He is not affected by anything that transpires in the world he has made.[9] In contrast, their view of God is that of a loving, caring parent. He experiences the world, interacts with his children, and feels emotions. He takes risks and, in response to developments in the world, changes his mind and his actions. He does not arbitrarily and unilaterally control the world. He shares that control with humans. He is a partner with them, rather than a tyrant. Unlike a God whose experience is closed because he knows and has determined everything that will happen, this kind of God has an open experience of the world.[10]

*Divine love.* In the open view of God, love is the central dimension, and love of a particular kind. Rice says, "love is the most important quality we attribute to God, and love is more than care and commitment; it involves being sensitive and responsive as well."[11] There is, therefore, genuine interaction between God and humans. He does not simply act in relation to them; he also reacts to what they do. Whereas in classical theism God's will is thought of as the sole cause of what occurs, here history is the combined result of God's working and humans' actions. This means that God does not act coercively, but by seeking to induce humans to act freely in agreement with his intentions for them. This is of the very nature of love. There is

---

9. Richard Rice, "Biblical Support for a New Perspective," in Clark Pinnock, Richard Rice, John Sanders, William Hasker, and David Basinger, *The Openness of God: A Biblical Challenge to the Traditional Understanding of God.* (Downers Grove, Ill.: InterVarsity, 1994), pp. 11–15.

10. Ibid., pp. 15–18

11. Ibid., p. 15.

a parallel here with the process conception of God "luring" rather than coercing. One major difference is seen in the basis of this relationship. For the free will theist, this is a limitation that God has freely chosen.[12] In process theology, on the other hand, the limitation appears to come from God's very nature.

If this is the case, however, then God's knowledge must also be understood in a different way than it is in classical theism. Instead of being static and completely formed in advance, God's knowledge is dynamic, for he comes to know what occurs as it happens. Thus, God's knowledge and experience are truly open, affected by new occurrences in the world.

These limitations should not be thought of as imperfections in God. He knows infallibly the past and the present, and all there is to know about the future. The future is not something that already exists, however, like a woven rug waiting to be unrolled. Rather, it is something that is being woven by humans and God through their free actions. And being free, those actions are contingent, and consequently cannot be known by God in advance.[13] Those in the classical theistic tradition would insist that God must have complete and perfect foreknowledge, and his failure in this regard is an imperfection. The free will theists contend that this is not the case. Their argument rests on a parallel between omniscience and omnipotence. Omnipotence means that God can do everything and anything, but this is usually qualified by a statement such as, "all things that are proper objects of power." God cannot do the logically impossible, such as making square circles. This is not considered a weakness or a threat to the doctrine of omnipotence, however, since the logically contradictory is not a true object of power. Such actions actually do not exist in reality, but only in the hypothetical realm of the imaginable. So, the future free actions of humans are not something that can be known, because they do not yet exist. God's inability to know them is not a threat to the doctrine of divine omniscience, any

12. Clark H. Pinnock, "Systematic Theology," in *The Openness of God*, p. 113; Gregory A. Boyd, in *Letters from a Skeptic*, by Gregory A. Boyd and Edward K. Boyd (Wheaton, Ill.: Victor, 1994), pp. 45–48.

13. Pinnock, "Systematic Theology," pp. 121–24; Boyd, *Letters*, pp. 30–31, 33.

more than his inability to make square circles is a valid objection to the doctrine of divine omnipotence.

Another parallel to process thought is seen in Rice's twofold conception of the being of God. In relationship to the temporal world, God's experience is progressive, developmental, and thus, open. There is, however, another dimension of God, in which he is unaffected by the world and incapable of or insusceptible to any type of development or change.[14] For example, with respect to his character, consider God's love. This is the way he is, and he cannot possibly be otherwise. It simply is part of his nature. This, and his other qualities, such as mercy, justice, and the like, are unaffected by anything that happens in the world.[15] This is sometimes expressed by saying that God is unchanged and unchanging in his nature, but his plans and actions, as well as his emotions and experience, alter. This sounds rather similar to the process understanding of God's nature as dipolar.

The most complete picture of the open view of God has been given us by Richard Rice. Since the open God is a God of relationship, we can understand him best by observing five of his relationships.

1. The openness of God and creation. God has created everything that is, including human beings. We must understand the total act of creation by understanding that God created humans in his own image (Gen. 1:26–27). Whereas classical theism often understood this image in terms of something substantive or structural within humans, the free will theists conceive of it functionally, in terms of what humans do, such as having dominion over the creation. So the understanding of the image of God is that the human also has and is to exercise this creative power over the universe. Rice says, "In creating man in His image and endowing him with dominion over the earth, God was, in effect, inviting man henceforth to participate with Him in the work of Creation. Or perhaps we should say that God intended to continue His creative activity through the agency of His creatures. At any rate, Genesis 2 presents us with the God who creates a world and gives it the capacity for

14. Rice, *God's Foreknowledge*, p. 26.
15. Ibid., p. 27.

self-creation."[16] The openness of creation refers to the capacity of God's creatures for further creative activity. It should not, however, be thought of as any sort of imperfection on God's part, for he did not need humans to make up for some failure on his own part. He simply chose to do it this way.[17]

2. The openness of God and human freedom. God has given humans genuine freedom, that is, the capacity to choose between genuine options, or the capacity to do other than one did. This means that God could not give the human the ability to obey without also giving the ability to disobey. Thus the future of the world was not fixed in advance. God created a genuinely open world.[18]

Such a conception of human moral freedom is believed to provide this view a great advantage over the traditional view, in terms of its ability to deal with the vexing problem of evil. A common solution to the problem of how there can be evil in a world created and ruled by an all-powerful and completely loving God is that he has created humans with free will, and they have used (or misused) this freedom, resulting in evil in the world. If, however, God has perfect foreknowledge, then he knew which humans would use their freedom to do evil and still chose to bring them into existence. Consequently, he is responsible for the evil that they could have done. He could have prevented this evil, but did not. So we still have the dilemma.[19]

For the free will theist, however, this is not a problem. For if the future is genuinely open, then God cannot know it until it occurs. He knew that humans *could* rebel, but not that they *would*. He is therefore only responsible for the possibility of evil, not for its reality. Humans are responsible for its actuality. So the open view solves the most serious intellectual problem of the Christian faith.[20]

3. The openness of God and the future. We have observed that these free will theists hold that the reason God does not know the future is because it is not yet there to be known. It is

16. Ibid., pp. 36–37.
17. Ibid., p. 37.
18. Ibid., p. 38.
19. Ibid., p. 50.
20. Ibid., pp. 51–52.

not fixed in advance. It is less like a rug that is unrolled as time goes by than it is like a rug that is being woven.

As we pointed out, the free will theists do not consider this an objection to the idea of omniscience, since there are things that are inherently unknowable, just as there are things that are intrinsically undo-able. Consequently, not knowing the future does not mean that God is lacking in knowledge. Rather, it means that "His knowledge corresponds precisely with what there is to know."[21]

This does not mean that God knows nothing about the future, however. The future is partially definite, not totally indefinite. Many of the things that will occur in the future are the result of past and present causes. Since God knows the past and present exhaustively, he can know the things that result. In addition, God knows what he is going to do in the future. Thus, the fact that he does not know the future in detail does not mean that he is completely ignorant of it.[22] In addition, he knows the range of possibilities of persons' actions, and what will be the consequences of each of these possibilities. So, although he does not know precisely what will occur, he knows what may, and, in each of the scenarios, what the result will be. While the future is open to God, it is not wide open.[23]

4. The openness of God and providence. The free will theists believe that God is at work in the world, accomplishing his purposes. He supports the natural order, and sometimes even departs from his customary and familiar manner of working (natural laws) to perform the unusual, or miracles. Beyond that, God is especially involved with human history, and sometimes even responds to events that would seem to thwart his purposes, to accomplish them nonetheless. The evil Joseph's brothers did to him and the stubbornness of Pharaoh are examples of this sort of working.[24]

The nature of God's providential working is conceived quite differently on the open view of God than traditionally. In classical theism God is seen as controlling everything through an

21. Ibid., pp. 54–55.
22. Ibid., p. 55.
23. Ibid., pp. 56–58.
24. Ibid., p. 62.

eternal decision to adopt a total plan. That pictures his relationship to the world and history to be now a relatively passive one. On the open model, however, the future becomes apparent to God as his human agents carry out their actions, and he responds to those actions, adjusting his working accordingly. It is important to distinguish between God's ultimate intentions for the world, which have been planned from eternity, and the actions he takes to implement these within time. When thought of in terms of his plan for the human race, it is apparent that God's general intention is that everyone should be saved, but this only comes to pass in each individual case as specific individuals accept that offer.[25]

5. The openness of God and prophecy. Some critics of the open view have felt that predictive prophecy must present an insuperable difficulty for it. After all, if God is able to predict what occurs, he must at least be able to know the future in all of its particularity, or even control it. How can God give predictive prophecy, if the future and his knowledge are really open?

There are various possibilities for accounting for given prophecies, according to free will theists. One is that the specific prophecy in question is actually an event that God knows, on the basis of his exhaustive knowledge of past and present factors, will inevitably come to pass. Others are expressions of God's intention to act in a certain way, and God certainly knows what he intends to do. Some prophecies may be a combination of these two factors.[26] In addition, some of them may be conditional prophecies, or declarations of God's intention to act in a certain way if a particular course of action occurs or if people behave in a certain way. One of the clearest examples of this latter type of prophecy would be Jonah's prophecy to Nineveh. In that case, the prophecy was a real declaration of Jehovah's intention to destroy Nineveh, which would surely have come to pass, *unless the people of Nineveh repented.* In fact, this warning was a means by which God would bring about that repentance. So, without knowing in advance what they would do, God was able to declare what he would do, unless they changed their behavior.[27]

25. Ibid., pp. 63–64.
26. Ibid., pp. 77–79.
27. Ibid., pp. 79–80.

We should note that this view is not as unique or esoteric as we might think. While this is a thoroughly worked out intellectual worldview, in practice it may underlie the thinking and acting of larger numbers of lay Christians. David Basinger, in his chapter on "Practical Implications," contends that this is the case. He even identifies Garry Friesen's book, *Decision Making and the Will of God*, with the position of John Sanders as somewhat more open than that of the other openness theologians regarding the definiteness of God's will.[28]

## The Argument for the Position

The case for the open view of God is most fully presented in the symposium, *The Openness of God*. Several lines of evidence are marshaled in a series of chapters by the five authors.

*Biblical.* Rice presents the biblical case for the open view. Essentially, he contends that this view better accords with the biblical evidence than does the alternative or traditional view. He acknowledges that those who hold the traditional view can marshal a rather large number of Scriptures in support of their position. That is not the issue, however, he argues. The question is rather which position best accords with the overall view of God, as that emerges from the variety of biblical materials. He asserts that despite being able to appeal to a number of biblical statements, the traditional view "does not reflect faithfully the spirit of the biblical message." While he does not intend to offer a detailed refutation of the conventional view, he sketches the open view and shows that this portrait is compatible with some passages that seem to call it into question.[29]

While there is a variety of biblical materials regarding God, it is important to note that most of the descriptions are metaphors, Rice contends. He intends to restore these metaphors to the prominence they deserve in our thinking, especially those that deal with divine suffering and divine repentance: "Giving such metaphors more weight will enable us to achieve an understanding of God that is much more faithful to the Bible than is the familiar alternative."[30] There are two lines of evidence

28. Basinger, *The Openness of God*, p. 201, n. 25.
29. Rice, "Biblical Support," p. 15.
30. Ibid., p. 17.

for the open view of God. One is the statements that affirm in one way or another that God responds to what happens in the world with certain emotions and changes in attitude or plans. The other involves statements that appear to affirm the freedom of humans in one way or another.[31]

The most important biblical affirmation about God is the statement that God is love (1 John 4:8). This is not just another attribution of a quality to God; rather, it is as close as the Bible comes to defining God: "Love is the essence of the divine reality, the basic source from which *all* of God's attributes arise."[32]

When Rice examines the Old Testament, he finds numerous attributions to God of a variety of feelings, including joy, grief, anger, and regret. The Book of Hosea is especially significant in this connection. There also are many statements about God repenting or changing his mind. Some of these are cases where God is sorry for what he has done, such as creating the human race (Gen. 6:6) or making Saul king (1 Sam. 15:35). Others are changes concerning what he has said he will do or has started to do, such as his decision not to destroy Nineveh, as he said he would. The New Testament also contains significant data regarding God's openness, especially in his becoming human and coming to the human race in the person of Jesus Christ as well as suffering.

*Historical considerations.* One might wonder why the chapter on the history of Christian thought by John Sanders is included as an argument for the open position, since it shows how prevalent the conventional view has been in the past. Sanders and his colleagues recognize that the conventional view seems quite compelling, even obvious to some Christians today, and the purpose of the chapter is to show why this is, namely, that because of the received tradition we misinterpret the Scriptures. The reason for this tradition departing from the true biblical picture is that the Greek view of God as immutable and impassible was progressively adopted by Christian theology.[33] The Reformers raised some questions about the tradi-

31. Ibid., p. 18.
32. Ibid., p. 21.
33. John Sanders, "Historical Considerations," in *The Openness of God*, p. 59.

tion, but basically maintained it. Even Jacob Arminius, while he significantly modified the traditional view, never saw any real conflict between some of his ideas and the doctrine of impassability.[34] In the modern period, theology has divided into three groups on the nature of God. Paul Tillich and the process theologians made major modifications of the classical view. The conservative theologians, such as Carl F. H. Henry and J. I. Packer, divide the understanding of God into the transcendent, as he is in himself, in which aspect he is immutable and impassable, and the immanent, God as he appears to us, in which he is changeable and responsive. Conservative piety and hymnody are quite different from conservative theology, however, depicting a responsive God who answers prayer. Finally, there are those such as the free will theists, who hold moderate views of God. Their numbers, both among theologians and philosophers, are growing.[35]

*Theological considerations.* Clark Pinnock reiterates many of the same ideas presented in the two previous chapters. His major contribution is in showing the theological difficulties that result from the synthesis of Greek philosophy with biblical teaching. Two areas especially illustrate this, namely, God's timelessness and his omniscience, understood as including foreknowledge.

Divine timelessness creates numerous theological problems. We cannot form any idea of timelessness, since all our thinking is temporally conditioned. Further, it creates problems for biblical history, since God seems to experience the flow of time and a future that is not completely settled. Moreover, it undermines our worship, because we praise God for his actions in time. Finally, a God who did not experience events as they occur would not be experiencing or knowing the actual world.[36]

Similar difficulties accompany the idea of God's perfect foreknowledge of all that will occur in the future. It does not accord with the biblical picture of a God who makes discoveries and professes ignorance of some matters. If God could not ex-

34. Ibid., pp. 60–91.
35. Ibid., pp. 91–98.
36. Pinnock, "Systematic Theology," in *The Openness of God,* p. 120.

perience surprise and delight, this would be a serious limitation on him, and such a world would be boring. Perhaps most
significant, however, is that if God knew what we were going to
do, it would be certain, and we would not be truly free.[37]

This latter point is extremely important, and is the reason
these theologians term themselves "free will theists." The argument had been raised by Pinnock earlier, but has now taken a
central place in the argument.[38] Traditional Arminians have held
that God knows the future, not because he has determined that
by his own causation, but because he foresees human actions. In
those varieties that hold to divine timelessness, the entire span of
time is immediately present to God, so that he is not really *fore-
seeing* it. Here, however, these Arminians take the argument a
step further. If God knows what humans are going to do, it must
be certain what they will do, or God would be mistaken. If it is
certain what I will do, however, I cannot do otherwise. I really am
not free, then, in the sense of being able to do otherwise. Thus,
since we know ourselves to be free, God must not know the future, insofar as that involves free human actions.

*Philosophical considerations.* William Hasker probes more
fully the issues of divine power, knowledge, and providential
governance. He contends that on these matters the open view
of God presents fewer philosophical difficulties than do any of
the alternatives. Especially with respect to conflict with human
freedom and the problem of evil, the superiority of the open
view can be seen.

*Practical considerations.* The argument by David Basinger is
primarily a pragmatic one: that the open view fits better with
the practical dimensions of the Christian life, as outlined in the
Bible, than does the classical view. This is seen in several areas.
Petitionary prayer does not fit with the classical view, since it
cannot affect what happens, if God has already determined
that. A God who responds to humans and even changes his
mind can be prayed to, however.[39] Similarly, with respect to

37. Ibid., pp. 121–23.
38. Pinnock, "God Limits His Knowledge," in *Predestination and Free Will:
Four Views of Divine Sovereignty and Human Freedom,* ed. David Basinger and
Randall Basinger (Downers Grove, Ill.: InterVarsity, 1986), pp. 156–59.
39. David Basinger, "Practical Implications," in *The Openness of God,* pp.
160–62.

discerning and doing God's will, the specific sovereignty view must really conclude that it does not matter, since whatever God wills occurs. The openness model, on the other hand, allows for seeking insight from God, since he knows the possibilities, but what humans do makes a difference.[40] In matters of human suffering, evangelistic responsibility, and social responsibility, the openness view avoids the passivity that follows logically from the traditional conception, and therefore is a better basis for practical Christian living.[41]

## Evaluation

This theology proposes some major changes in the form of understanding of God that has been prevalent for much of the church's history. As such, it deserves careful evaluation, in terms of both its values and its dangers.

### Positive

1. The attempt to be genuinely biblical is a commendable goal for those who term themselves evangelicals.
2. There is a genuine effort to treat the doctrine of God in a thorough fashion, doing genuine systematic theology. This involves use of the biblical sources, consultation of the history of the doctrine, scrutiny in light of philosophical categories, and attention to practical issues. It attempts to fulfill the objectives that several recent evangelical theologies have set for themselves.[42]
3. The concern for the practical dimensions of the doctrine is commendable, since theology is not an end in itself but is to be a source of nurture for the Christian church.
4. The concern for context is important. All theology is done from some point within history, and needs to be expressed in a form that will be meaningful and understandable to its primary audience. Whether we accept

40. Ibid., pp. 166–68.
41. Ibid., pp. 168–76.
42. E.g., Gordon Lewis and Bruce Demarest, *Integrative Theology* (Grand Rapids: Zondervan, 1987), vol. 1, pp. 7–9, 21–58. Millard Erickson, *Christian Theology* (Grand Rapids: Baker, 1986), pp. 59–80.

the intellectual and cultural dimensions of a given context, we cannot ignore it without the danger of our theology becoming irrelevant.

5. Conversely, however, there is the importance of ascertaining that a given theology is not simply dominated by the spirit of the time. There is real substance in the warning against allowing the biblical witness to be distorted by a philosophy, as these theologians maintain has occurred with respect to Greek philosophy.

## Negative

1. The biblical undergirding is questionable in a number of ways. The Scriptures used are carefully selected. While everyone does use some sort of hermeneutical motif in interpreting passages and making hermeneutical value judgments, these should fit with the total evidence of Scripture. There is extremely little attention given to passages that speak of the holiness, wrath, and judgment of God. If one is to rely on the broad sweep of Scripture, then those motifs should be demonstrably biblical at some specific points.

2. Some passages of Scripture conflict with this open view of God, and the explanations given of them by the openness theologians are not adequate. One of these is the large amount of predictive prophecy in the Bible, much of it rather specifically detailed. Rice recognizes the problem, and explains prophecy in terms of three considerations: God's declaration of what he will do; God's prediction on the basis of certain fixed factors, such as physical laws; and the conditional nature of some of the prophecies, such as the threat to destroy Nineveh. This explanation tends to be rather insufficient, however, since some of the prophecies involved specific human actions that would be very difficult to predict on the basis of present knowledge of causes and trends in place. Examples of these would be Jesus' prophecies regarding the actions of Peter and Judas.

Another major area of difficulty pertains to the passages regarding God repenting, which are interpreted with a very literal hermeneutic. There are, however, at least two passages that specifically state that God does not repent, namely, Numbers 23:19 and 1 Samuel 15:29. Rice's reply is that these are actually saying that God does not lie, but closer examination of the passages in question renders that interpretation highly suspect. A better harmonization of the data would be to interpret the references to God repenting in light of these clear didactic passages, and to take the former as anthropomorphisms and anthropopathisms instead.

3. The argument that the classical view derives from Greek thought suffers at a number of points. First, it seems to rest on the contention of the biblical theology movement that the true biblical view was Hebraic, as contrasted with Greek. This conception has been largely discredited, however, especially by the work of James Barr.[43] Further, the assessment of the history of Christian thought tends to overlook the indications that the classical view did not follow the Thomistic model in all respects, as shown, for example, in Luther's reference to the suffering God.[44] And an examination of recent evangelical theologies indicates a much less Greek view of God on such topics as divine impassability than the openness theologians impute to orthodox theology.[45]

4. The rejection of divine foreknowledge on the basis of its conflict with human freedom assumes an incompatibilist view of freedom. While the opposite view, that certainty about what will happen is compatible with genuine human freedom, is acknowledged, it is not really refuted.

5. Although this approach claims to have solved the problem of evil, what it really has dealt with is what I term

43. James Barr, *The Semantics of Biblical Language* (London: Oxford University Press, 1961). Cf. Brevard S. Childs, *Biblical Theology in Crisis* (Philadelphia: Westminster, 1970), p. 72.

44. Alistair E. McGrath, "Whatever Happened to Luther?" *Christianity Today* 39.1 (January 9, 1995): 34.

45. E.g., Lewis and Demarest, *Integrative Theology*, pp. 235–37; Erickson, Christian Theology, p. 270; Wayne Grudem, *Systematic Theology: An Introduction to Biblical Doctrine* (Grand Rapids: Zondervan, 1994), pp. 165–66.

"the problem of the problem of evil." That is, it has offered a resolution of the question, "How can a loving
and all-powerful God allow evil in the world?" It does
not really handle the more serious problem, which
could more accurately be termed the problem of evil
proper, namely, "Will evil be overcome?" If God does
not coerce humans, but allows them to exercise their
free wills, even to contravene his will, what assurance
is there that God's cause will ultimately triumph?
Hasker seems to suggest that if necessary to ensure the
victory of good, God can intervene to override the
human will.[46] If this is the case, however, then the difference between their view and the classical one is not
one of kind but of degree. It is not whether God co-
erces, but how frequently he does so, and presumably,
on their terms, either is undesirable. And, for that matter, the former problem is not really solved by the free
will defense. For if God freely chose to limit himself by
creating free human beings, could he not have chosen
otherwise, and is he not therefore at least partially and
indirectly culpable?

6. The practical efficacy of the open view of God is less
   clear than they would contend. For example, does it really avail to pray for something to occur in the lives of
   free persons, if that requires human choices, and if God
   does not "coerce"? And what good is it to seek guidance
   from a God who does not really know large portions of
   the future?

7. There are rhetorical problems at a number of points in
   the argument. One is the use of pejorative language,
   such as "a puppet-master controlling the movements of
   a puppet," "a ventriloquist having a 'conversation' with
   his dummy," and "a computer wizard who has assem-
   bled a lifelike robot," to describe the Calvinistic view.[47]
   This type of caricature is not worthy of a presumably
   scholarly work, especially when used by a skilled philosopher such as Hasker. There also are logical gaps

46. Hasker, "A Philosophical Perspective," p. 142.
47. Ibid., pp. 142–43.

and leaps in the argument, such as Rice's movement from "These considerations suggest that" to "Apparently, then . . ." without intervening evidence.[48]

8. Finally, we have commended these theologians for their recognition of the effect of historical conditioning on theologies and other ideologies. Unfortunately, however, this insight seems to be restricted to their analysis of the classical view, and does not extend to their own. There is an amazing lack of acknowledgment, or even recognition, of the place that philosophical and other presuppositions play in their theology. Rather than acknowledging that their acceptance of contemporary ideas relativizes their view, this is made a virtue, demonstrating the relevance of their open view.[49]

48. Rice, "God's Foreknowledge," p. 36.
49. E.g., Pinnock, "Systematic Theology," p. 107.

# 5 The Doctrine of Salvation

**The** doctrine of salvation has been a topic of strong interest in recent years for evangelicals, in part because it has always been so central to their theology and life. By the very nature of evangelical faith, and as the name of the movement indicates, evangelicals have emphasized the proclamation of the gospel. Evangelism and missions have been key to the life of the evangelical church, and have contributed to the growth of evangelical churches and denominations, at a time when other segments of Christianity have plateaued or declined.

Much of the discussion in recent years has centered on the basis and extent of salvation, or, to put it another way, the question of whether those who are not explicit Christians (who have not heard the message of Jesus Christ, and consciously placed their faith and trust in him and his saving work) may be saved. A related topic is the question of how many will be saved—whether many or relatively few.

## The Traditional View and Challenges to It

By the late nineteenth and early twentieth centuries, a fairly uniform position had been adopted by evangelicals. The major points of the doctrine of salvation included the following:

1. God is a perfectly holy being, untouched by sin or temptation. Since he created humans to have fellowship with him, he expects them to be as perfectly holy as he is.
2. All humans are sinners, by both action and disposition. Not only do they perform sinful acts, but they have sin-

109

    ful natures. No one is righteous in God's sight, and no one can do anything to qualify for salvation.

3. The only basis for salvation is the sinless life, atoning death, and resurrection of Jesus Christ.
4. The reception of this salvation is only through conscious belief in Christ.
5. Death ends the opportunity for accepting this salvation. The relationship one has with Christ at the moment of death is eternally fixed.
6. All those who believe in Christ receive salvation in this life and spend eternity in heaven, in God's presence. All others are condemned to hell, a place of unending eternal anguish and suffering.

There were, of course, variations on these themes. Calvinists believed that those who were to be saved had been chosen by God's eternal act of election, while Arminians held that there is no such thing as unconditional predestination. Because all humans have free will, anyone who chooses may be saved.

There also was some variation on the question of the number saved. In general, evangelicals held that only a relatively small number of those who have lived will be saved, but some postmillennialists, such as B. B. Warfield, believed that the gospel would be preached successfully, so that a large number—perhaps the majority—of humans will be saved.[1]

The view of the traditionally sacramental churches, particularly the Roman Catholic Church, included an additional element. Not only was it necessary to be aware of Jesus and to be a believer in him, but one also had to be connected to the church in some official way. This was because grace was believed to be dispensed through the sacraments, and only a communicant Christian, or in other words, a member in good standing of the Church, could partake of these sacraments. This was expressed in the classic Roman Catholic formula, "outside the church, no salvation."

There have always been some who departed from this basic cluster of beliefs. As early as the third century, Origen pro-

---

1. B. B. Warfield, "Are They Few that Be Saved?" in *Biblical and Theological Studies* (Philadelphia: Presbyterian and Reformed, 1952), pp. 334–50.

pounded the idea of *apokatastasis*, the conception that all things will be reconciled to God and that consequently all persons will be saved. This was one of the earliest instances of universalism, which has become quite prominent in the nineteenth and twentieth centuries and, on a popular and emotional level, is perhaps quite widespread. This actually is in some ways a rather conservative view, since it basically holds that Christianity is the true religion, but that the Christian God will in some way bring all persons into proper relationship with him.

Probably the more widely held view in the latter part of the twentieth century, however, is pluralism, the belief that there are many ways of salvation. Salvation is not restricted to Christians, but one may be saved through adherence to other world religions as well. There are two varieties of pluralism. One in effect says that all religions are really the same. Although they may contain different doctrines, they all involve the same sort of experience. The other concedes that there are significant differences among the world religions, but they are alternative routes to God.

There are a number of reasons why there has come to be dissatisfaction with the older, more restrictive view.

1. The anthropological. Greater mobility and globalization have brought Christians in contact with devotees of other great religions. Unlike the strange "pagans" that they were once thought to be, these are found to be good, moral people. The question naturally arises, "How can God reject or damn persons like this, just because they do not happen to believe in Jesus?"
2. The emotional. The idea of a loving and just God condemning people who do not believe in Jesus simply because they have never heard of him and consequently have really had no opportunity to believe, is offensive to sensitive, caring people. This is particularly so with respect to the idea of hell as an endless suffering. There simply must be some other way.
3. The exegetical. There are some passages, particularly in the letters of Paul, that sound strongly universalistic, such as 1 Corinthians 15:22 and Colossians 1:20. To be

true to the view of authority and hermeneutics usually espoused by evangelicals presents some real difficulty for the traditional exclusivist view in attempting to deal with these passages.

4. The general cultural. There is a strong tendency toward relativism, in which all views are regarded as equally true, whether in religion, philosophy, or some other area. Part of this is reflected in the "evangelical civility," in which one must not tell anyone that they are wrong, or certainly that they are sinners and even bound for hell.

## The Postconservative Evangelical View of Salvation

A final challenge to the traditional view is inclusivism. This is the idea that Christianity is the true religion, and that salvation is only through the work of Jesus Christ, but that more persons may be included in these benefits than had traditionally been thought. It may be that some are saved by Christ's work but without consciously believing in Christ. It is in this category that the postconservative evangelical view of salvation falls.

*Implicit faith.* The postconservative evangelicals have emphasized a number of ideas with respect to salvation. One of these is the doctrine of implicit faith, or salvation through the knowledge of God from general revelation. This is not something new with these evangelicals. The idea was present in the thought of some other evangelicals earlier in the twentieth century, such as Augustus Hopkins Strong[2] and Sir Norman Anderson.[3] It has been pursued at greater length by these theologians, however.

Inclusivism rests on the belief in the reality of general revelation. Pinnock notes that evangelicals have generally recognized the reality and value of general revelation, yet have been reluctant to grant the possibility of anyone being saved through

2. Augustus Hopkins Strong, *Systematic Theology* (Westwood, N.J.: Revell, 1907), pp. 842–44.

3. Norman Anderson, *Christianity and World Religions: The Challenge of Pluralism* (Downers Grove, Ill.: InterVarsity, 1984), pp. 146–55.

this. He notes a strange paradox: that evangelicals have not hesitated to draw on the insights of philosophers in constructing their theologies and apologetics, but have not been similarly generous in their assessment of the thought of founders and other leaders of great world religions other than Christianity. He asks, "Why do we look so hopefully to Plato and expect nothing from Buddha?"[4] The postconservatives hold to the validity of general revelation because of several factors.

1. There is considerable biblical testimony regarding the efficacy of general revelation. Evangelicals have sometimes depreciated general revelation out of a sense of loyalty to special revelation, and the belief that to give validity to general revelation would be to rob special revelation of its value. This does not follow, however, says Sanders. Inclusivists, such as Pinnock and himself, see general revelation as one means by which God makes himself known savingly to humans. It is God who is doing the revealing; it is not a human accomplishment. General revelation is, therefore, salvific because its source is God. Indeed, knowledge of God is always saving in nature. It is, of course, not general revelation that does the saving. It is merely a means by which God saves. May it be, as some contend, that the purpose of general revelation is only to condemn or to make people guilty? Pinnock does not think this could be the case. He quotes with approval the statement of Dale Moody, who questions what kind of a God would make enough known about himself to make persons guilty, but not to save them. Rather, people can be saved or lost, depending on their response to general revelation.[5] Texts that testify of this revelation to all humans are Acts 14:17; Psalm 19:1; and Romans 10:18.

Sanders is careful to protect the inclusivist understanding of general revelation against possible misunderstandings. The first consideration is that this does not in any sense represent a depreciation of special revelation. Rather, these theologians are simply insisting on the fact of God seeking humans through this channel.

4. Clark Pinnock, "The Finality of Jesus Christ in a World of Religions," in *Christian Faith and Practice in the Modern World: Theology from an Evangelical Point of View*, ed. Mark A. Noll and David F. Wells (Grand Rapids: Eerdmans, 1988), p. 159.

5. Sanders, *No Other Name*, p. 233.

Further, one can only really understand the truth of special revelation against the background of general revelation. For example,
special revelation tells us of the importance of a relationship to
God, but we know of the reality of that God through general revelation. Second, he wants to make clear that it is indeed God's revelation, not a human discovery. Third, this is in no sense a matter
of salvation by human works. Just as no Jews were ever able to fulfill the requirements of the Mosaic Law through their own efforts,
so no one can by personal accomplishment fulfill the Law known
from nature. Fourth, this does not represent a denial of the sinfulness of all humans. Romans and other biblical testimonies of universal human sinfulness are taken at face value.[6]

2. There are other biblical texts that do not speak directly of
general revelation, but from which the inference of God's general revelation follows. These are of several types. One group
speaks of God's desire to see all persons saved. These include
such texts as 1 Timothy 1:15; 4:10; John 3:16–17; 12:32; 2 Peter
3:9; and Matthew 7:23.

3. Another large group of relevant texts are those that speak
of God's special concern for Gentiles. Deuteronomy mentions
God providing land for several nations by driving out other
peoples (2:5, 9, 19, 21–22), and Amos seems to indicate that
God provided feats similar to the exodus of Israel from Egypt
(9:7) for other nations.

4. There are also several instances in the Old Testament
where God seemed not to restrict his favor to those within the
Abrahamic covenant. These Gentiles lived either before that
covenant was established, or after it, but came from outside the
nation of Israel. Among these were Abel, Enoch, Lot, Job, Bal-
aam, the Queen of Sheba, Ruth, Melchizedek, Jethro, Rahab,
and Naaman. Other indications of knowledge of God by those
outside the covenant are Cyrus, Nebuchadnezzar, and the
pagan sailors in the Book of Jonah.

This is evidence for there being another covenant, in addition to the Abrahamic covenant, a covenant with all persons.
This is the Noachic covenant, made with "all flesh" (Gen. 9:8–
19).[7] Pinnock sees this as an indication of God's saving purpose

6. Ibid., pp. 234–36.
7. Ibid., p. 219.

for and activity with people: "By this pledge we understand that God is concerned, not with a single strand of history, but with the entire historical tapestry, including all the earth's peoples. God announces in this covenant that his saving purposes are going to be working, not just among a single chosen nation but among all peoples sharing a common ancestry to Noah."[8]

5. Most important are the New Testament references to Gentiles who apparently were included within the scope of God's salvation. Melchizedek is mentioned by the writer of Hebrews as the priest of the true God, and even one in whose order Jesus has become a high priest (6:20–7:18). Beyond that, however, there is the interesting incident involving Cornelius. Here was a Gentile who experienced the full salvation that had come to Jews. Pinnock says of him, "Like Job in the Old Testament, here was a Gentile in a good and acceptable relationship with God."[9]

6. Pinnock sees the Cornelius account as one of several indications of Luke's openness to Gentiles. This is combined with a strong commitment to the uniqueness and finality of Jesus Christ in Luke's writing in the Book of Acts. Another example would be Luke's account of Paul's message to the Athenian philosophers at the Areopagus.[10]

7. Empirical instances form a further source for these inclusivists' argument. Pinnock cites with approval Don Richardson's book, *Eternity in Their Hearts*. Richardson describes numerous tribes of people whose beliefs prior to the coming of the missionaries with the gospel message showed considerable similarities to the content of that message.[11] He also notes C. S. Lewis's *The Last Battle*, which although fiction, shows Lewis's belief in the efficacy of general revelation. He also cites some examples of his own of those who he believes have known much about God from general revelation alone. He notes, for example, Gautama Buddha, "whose ethical direction, compassion and concern for others

8. Clark H. Pinnock, *A Wideness in God's Mercy: The Finality of Jesus Christ in a World of Religions* (Grand Rapids: Zondervan, 1992), p. 21.

9. Ibid., p. 95.

10. Pinnock, "The Finality of Jesus Christ," p. 158.

11. Don Richardson, *Eternity in Their Hearts* (Ventura, Calif.: Regal, 1984), pp. 73–102.

is so moving that it appears God is at work in his life." He believes that the idea of the impersonality of the ultimate reality in Buddha's thought has been overemphasized. While granting that Buddhism is not Christianity and does not try to be, he asks, "But how does one come away after encountering Buddhism and deny that it is in touch with God in its way?"[12] Similarly, he finds in the theistic Saiva Siddhanta literature of Hinduism, the Japanese Shi-Shu Amida sect, and the writings of Muhammed considerable similarities to Christian thought. He comments: "Religions do not present only the way of human self-justification. At times they also announce the grace and love of God. When they do, this Christian, at least, rejoices."[13]

8. One's hermeneutical stance is of prime importance to the issues, according to Pinnock. We must decide whether we will follow a hermeneutic of optimism or of pessimism. He believes that much evangelical thought on the subject has been dominated by a hermeneutic of pessimism. Those who adopt such an attitude emphasize the passages about the importance of faith in Christ, especially about the sinfulness and blindness of humans apart from Christ. They interpret very literally any passage suggesting that only few will be saved, such as Matthew 7:14, which is what he calls the "fewness doctrine." The real culprit in much of this pessimistic outlook is, in Pinnock's judgment, Augustine, who misunderstood and misconstrued the doctrine of election by making it a matter of individual salvation, rather than a vocation on behalf of the world.[14]

Rather, Pinnock suggests that there needs to be a shift to a whole new paradigm, the hermeneutic of hopefulness. He finds adequate basis for this approach in passages that suggest that large numbers of persons will be saved. In addition to those already noted, additional specific texts that seem to indicate that God wants to and even will, have mercy upon all people, include 1 Timothy 2:4 and Romans 11:32.[15]

12. *Wideness in God's Mercy*, p. 100.
13. Ibid., pp. 100–101.
14. Ibid., pp. 25, 37–43.
15. Ibid., pp. 18–19.

9. Of special importance in one's hermeneutic is the role of what these theologians call "control beliefs." These are fundamental conceptions consulted in one's interpretational decisions. Pinnock defines a control belief as "a large-scale conviction that affects many smaller issues."[16] The most significant of these is the understanding one has of God. He says, "The foundation of my theology of religions is a belief in the unbounded generosity of God revealed in Jesus Christ."[17] What kind of a God are we talking about? That is the fundamental question in such discussions. Is he the kind of God who sits by while large numbers of people perish, or does he tirelessly seek out sinners? Does he enjoy damning sinners, or is he appalled at the prospect?[18]

Similarly, Sanders speaks of theological considerations, and lists five basic theological arguments put forth in support of inclusivism. Actually, they are of the nature of Pinnock's control beliefs, and are theological presuppositions within which this theological theory is worked out.

1. Believers versus Christians. The inclusivists draw a crucial distinction between believers and Christians, which is frequently overlooked by some who discuss the issues. It is usually connected with the issue of faithful Gentiles. Sanders says: "In this context, believers can be defined as those who are saved because they have faith in God. Inclusivists contend that all Christians are believers but that not all believers are Christians. They define a Christian as a believer who knows about and participates in the work of Jesus Christ."[19] Believers would include Old Testament saints, who had the same salvation as New Testament believers do and appropriate it in the same way, namely, through faith. These are saved by means of Christ.[20] In view of this latter statement, it would seem that Sanders perhaps misstated himself, in apparently restricting participation in the work of Christ to Christians. It would seem that he meant to say that both believers and Christians participate in Christ's

16. Ibid., p. 18.
17. Ibid.
18. Ibid.
19. Sanders, *No Other Name*, pp. 224–25.
20. Ibid., pp. 225–27.

work, but Christians also believe in Christ, whereas believers believe in God.

2. The role of general revelation is a key factor, as we have discussed above. General revelation is a means by which God communicates himself to all persons, and it can have saving efficacy.[21]

3. The work of God in effecting salvation. Inclusivists see God the Father as loving all persons and desiring their salvation, God the Son as making this possible for all persons through his redemptive work, and God the Holy Spirit as working to convict all persons so that they respond to this universal offer of salvation. They insist that the Holy Spirit works with all persons, endeavoring to enable them to respond to whatever revelation they have available to them. Thus, even though the unevangelized are unreached by any human messenger, they are not unreached by the work of the Holy Spirit.

4. The cosmic work of Jesus Christ. This means that these theologians take seriously John 1:9, and interpret this as meaning that Christ existed and was enlightening people prior to his incarnation. While the incarnation constituted the supreme revelation of the Son of God, it was not the only one.

5. The implications of the presence of other religions. The inclusivists believe that at some points other religions have true understanding and belief about the true God. While the Christian biblical revelation is the norm by which all other claims to religious truth are judged, it is not the only one. The biblical writers did not hesitate to take the names for God from other religions (*El* and *theos*). The inclusivists note from Paul's message in Acts 17 that the Athenians did apparently at some point worship the true God.

The upshot of all these considerations is that in the judgment of the inclusivists, there is not only the possibility of persons who have not received special revelation being saved, but that significant numbers of persons are actually so saved. If the Old Testament believers could be saved without knowing the details of God's provision for their salvation, then why should not those who chronologically happen to live after Christ but epistemologically are before Christ be saved in the same fash-

21. Ibid., p. 233.

ion? They are not saved by works, but by faith in the grace of God. They do not know God through their own efforts enabling them to discover God, but they know him from his general revelation in nature and the human conscience.

A number of evangelical theologians, like J. I. Packer, believe that salvation is possible on this basis, but are uncertain how many, if any, are actually so saved. Pinnock, in particular, is quite critical of such persons. They are pictured as hoarding the grace of God, as stingy, niggardly with that grace, as if they were unwilling for persons to be saved. Pinnock even questions the right of such persons to be called evangelical.[22] He is much more optimistic. In response to the question of how many will be saved through this means, he professes that he does not know precisely, but that he hopes for multitudes of such.[23] The pictures in the Book of Revelation of large crowds around the throne suggest this.[24]

This does not mean that the gospel is not to be preached, however. There is no justification here for neglecting the missionary effort. Even though believers may be saved, it is still important for them to become Christians. There are dimensions of the fullness of experience involved in conscious trust in Jesus that are not available to the mere "believer."

*Postmortem encounter.* A somewhat different position has sometimes been taken as an alternative to the inclusivist or implicit faith position. In Pinnock's theology, however, it is combined with that conception. This is the view that those who do not have an opportunity during this life to hear the gospel will be given such an opportunity after death. This is sometimes known as "eschatological evangelism" or "postmortem encounter."

This view has had some support during various periods of the history of the church. It has traditionally been based on two considerations. One is the item in later versions of the Apostles' Creed that says that Jesus "descended into Hades." The other is 1 Peter 3:17–19 and 4:6, which reads:

22. Pinnock, *Wideness,* p. 163
23. "Finality of Jesus Christ," p. 164.
24. *Wideness*, p. 153.

For Christ also died for sins once for all, the righteous for the un-
righteous, that he might bring us to God, being put to death in
the flesh but made alive in the spirit; in which he went and
preached to the spirits in prison, who formerly did not obey,
when God's patience waited in the days of Noah, during the
building of the ark, in which a few, that is, eight persons, were
saved through water. (3:18–20)

For this is why the gospel was preached even to the dead, that
though judged in the flesh like men, they might live in the spirit
like God. (4:6)

Pinnock interprets this passage as teaching that Jesus, between his death on the cross and his resurrection, descended
into the realm of the dead and there proclaimed the Good News
of the offer of salvation to Old Testament persons who were im-
prisoned there. He further maintains that this justifies the belief that Jesus will give a similar opportunity to those who have
not had a chance during this life to hear.[25]

A first consideration in support of this contention is that
there are some whose fate is not sealed by death. The most notable instances of this would be those who die in infancy.
They are given some sort of opportunity beyond this life. Such
opportunity is not restricted to infants, however, in Pinnock's
judgment. This question is sometimes put in terms of whether
there are persons who qualify for such an opportunity. It is
not so much a matter of qualification, however, as it is of disposition. He says: "Humanity will appear in its entirety before
God and God has not changed from love to hate. Anyone
wanting to love God who has not loved him before is certainly
welcome to do so. It has not suddenly become forbidden. No,
the variable is the condition of the human souls appearing in
God's presence."[26]

This is an interesting argument, which seems to open the
door a bit wider than Pinnock proposes. If anyone who has not
previously loved God is allowed to do so at this point, what
about those who may have heard the gospel previously but
have not responded positively to it? Are they also among those

25. Pinnock, "Finality of Jesus Christ," p. 164.
26. Pinnock, *Wideness*, p. 171.

who could respond with love at this point, as well as those who have never heard? If the issue is not qualification but disposition, this would seem to be a genuine possibility.

There is another logical point involved in Pinnock's reasoning here. The concept of God, mentioned earlier as the supreme control belief, enters in at this point. The justice of God means that he would not condemn someone without the opportunity for that person to hear and believe, or at least, God knowing how the person would have responded in such a situation: "God, since he loves humanity, would not send anyone to hell without first ascertaining what their response would have been to his grace. Since everyone eventually dies and comes face to face with the risen Lord, that would seem to be the obvious time to discover their answer to God's call."[27]

But does God have to provide such an opportunity? Because he is omniscient, would he not know this without performing this sort of "experiment"? In Pinnock's view, however, as we saw in chapter 4, God does not know contingent human decisions and actions in advance of our making them. Thus, this opportunity must be given.

Pinnock is aware of the difficulty of the Peter passages. In light of this difficulty, some have thought that it would be best simply to suspend judgment. This is not Pinnock's stance, however: "In my view they are unduly cautious. The fact of God's universal salvific will coupled with several broad hints about the postmortem probation are enough for me to hope for such a thing."[28]

There is some ambiguity in Pinnock's thought as to just who will be given this opportunity. At some points, it sounds as if all persons who have not heard during this life will hear.[29] At another place, however, Pinnock seems to indicate that the opportunity for this postmortem hearing depends on the response to general revelation. He enumerates those who will likely have this opportunity for a postmortem encounter, and lists those who have been seeking for God and Jews who believed before Christ came. He says, "The exegetical evidence

27. Ibid., pp. 168–69.
28. Pinnock, "The Finality of Jesus Christ," p. 166.
29. *Wideness*, pp. 168–69; "Finality," p. 165.

may not be plentiful, but the theological argument is strong that those who have been seeking God in this life will have their knowledge of God updated when they enter into his presence."[30] On that reading of Pinnock, those who have made good use of the opportunity they have and made a positive response to it are given this more complete message. The logic of the idea that God must be able to determine what people would have done with the message, had they heard it, leads to the conclusion that it must be all who have not heard that get this opportunity, not merely those who have made some sort of positive response to general revelation.

Sanders mentions other texts often cited in support of this view. One of these is the fact that according to Revelation 21:25, the gates of the heavenly Jerusalem are never closed. He believes that this, when combined with texts indicating that many will come from all corners of the earth, means that the opportunity for salvation does not cease with death.[31]

But what of biblical texts that apparently assert that the gap between the saved and the unsaved is fixed at death? The major text usually appealed to here is Luke 16:19–31, where Jesus speaks of the great gulf fixed between the the rich man and Lazarus, so that no one can cross from one to the other. Does this not settle the matter? Sanders does not think so, and questions the interpretation that makes this parable germane to the discussion. He says, "so literalistic an interpretation is by no means generally accepted in the scholarly community, especially in light of the fact that the point of all three parables in Luke 16 is to instruct us about the use of wealth, not about eschatology."[32] Rather, the issue is which view "makes best sense of God's universal salvific will and the other guiding themes of Scripture." The verses such as this cited to support the fixity of one's status at death can quite easily be handled by the advocate of eschatological evangelization. At the very least, one would have to say that the biblical witness is unclear.[33] Thus, we have here a case of the use of a control belief, namely, the

30. *Wideness*, p. 172.
31. *No Other Name*, p. 191.
32. Ibid., n. 32.
33. Ibid., p. 209.

universal salvific will of God, to determine the interpretation of a passage that is in dispute.

Actually, the Peter passage does not directly address the question of those who have lived since the time of Christ. If the interpretation offered by the postconservatives here is correct, an additional step in the argument is needed, extending that opportunity to this group. Neither Pinnock nor Sanders really addresses this issue. About the closest to such a response is Pinnock's citation of Cranfield's statement about the descent passage: "it is a hint too that those who in subsequent ages have died without ever having had a real chance to believe in Christ are not outside the scope of his mercy and will not perish eternally without being given in some way that is beyond our knowledge an opportunity to hear the gospel and accept him as their Savior."[34] Beyond that, the argument seems to rest on the theological consideration.

*Annihilation.* The final area of discussion regarding the number who will be saved, and the way in which they are saved, is the idea of annihilation. This is the idea that those who do not come to saving faith, either in this life or beyond, will not suffer an endless punishment, but will simply cease to be. This is probably the most widespread of the modifications of the traditional position. There seems to have been a fairly significant number of British evangelicals who have adopted this position, among them John Stott, John Wenham, Michael Green, Stephen Travis, and Philip Edgecumbe Hughes. In the United States, the most complete argument for annihilation among evangelicals has been offered by Clark Pinnock. There are other indications of a more broadly based acceptance of this concept by American evangelicals.

Historically, there have been two major types of views of annihilationism. There has also been a third view, not widely held among Christians, called pure mortalism. This is the idea that humans are simply mortal, incapable of surviving death, so that death is the end of life. More popular are conditional immortality and annihilationism proper.

---

34. C. E. B. Cranfield, "The Interpretation of 1 Peter 3:19 and 4:6," *Expository Times* 69 (1958): 378. Quoted in Pinnock, *Wideness*, p. 169.

Conditional immortality is the idea that the human does not have any inherent powers of immortality. If the human is to survive death, it must be by a special act of God in conferring eternal life. Thus, those who die apart from Christ simply cease to be at death, or else at some point in the future, they simply "wear out." This view holds that the concept of the immortality of the soul is not a biblical and properly Christian idea, deriving instead from other sources. Annihilationism proper is the view that God, either at death, following the final judgment, or after a certain amount of punishment, takes some action to terminate the person.

A number of arguments are advanced in support of this view. Pinnock begins his most extended discussion of the subject by noting that all Christian doctrines have undergone some development throughout history, and eschatology is one of those doctrines. Consequently, all doctrinal formulations reflect some historical and cultural conditioning, and matters of eschatology are no different. In particular, he believes that in this area, as in so many others, it was Augustine who gave an unfortunate twist to the teaching of Scripture, resulting in this horrible doctrine of hell.[35] He recognizes that those who reject the traditional form of the doctrine will be accused of heresy, but he wants to counter that by showing that the traditional doctrine of hell is not biblically and theologically sound.[36]

Pinnock especially aims to rebut the idea that to fail to believe in hell is to fail to accept the Bible's teaching. The first argument is that the biblical picture of the future of the unbelieving is that of destruction, not of endless punishment. The language used to depict this future condition speaks of death, destruction, ruin, and perishing. Especially, the images of fire and destruction together suggest annihilation rather than torture, for the image is of fire consuming, rather than torturing, what is thrown into it.[37]

Pinnock finds abundant biblical support for this idea. Psalm 37, for example, says of the wicked that they wither like the

35. Pinnock, "The Destruction of the Finally Impenitent," *Criswell Theological Review* 4.2 (Spring 1990): 243–44.

36. Ibid., p. 250.

37. Ibid.

herb (v. 2), will be cut off and be no more (vv. 9–10), will perish and vanish like smoke (v. 20), and will be altogether destroyed (v. 38). A similar idea is found in Malachi 4:1. Jesus spoke of God, who could destroy both body and soul in hell (Matt. 10:28). John the Baptist said that the wicked are like dry wood to be thrown into the fire and like chaff to be burned (Matt. 3:10, 12). Jesus said that the wicked will be burned up like weeds thrown into the fire (Matt. 13:30, 42, 49–50). Paul said that God will destroy the wicked (1 Cor. 3:17; Phil. 1:28) and spoke of the end of the wicked as destruction (Phil. 3:19). Similar references are found in the General Epistles. Pinnock contends that it is not his view, but the traditional view for which supporting texts are in short supply.[38]

2. Pinnock also rejects the idea that there is an immortal element in humans that would have to be terminated. Rather, he says, the immortality of the soul is foreign to biblical revelation. It is derived from Greek philosophy. So there is no biblical basis for concluding that there would be survival beyond death, requiring any action by God. Instead, if God simply does nothing, the person would cease to exist. While Pinnock does not call his view conditional immortality, that is a necessary, but not sufficient, condition of his position. The reason is that it is still possible that God could give the wicked immortality, even if they do not inherently possess it.[39]

3. If the first point is biblical and the second is philosophical, the third is theological. It stems from the control belief of the idea of a good God. What kind of God would create persons, only to send them to an endless torture? Pinnock says that such a view "makes God into a bloodthirsty monster who maintains an everlasting Auschwitz for victims whom he does not even allow to die."[40] He also says that such a God "is more nearly like Satan than like God."[41]

There are, of course, advocates of the traditional view who, seeing its horrible character, try to modify the understanding. B. B. Warfield, for example, suggested that most will be saved,

38. Ibid., pp. 251–52.
39. Ibid., p. 253.
40. Ibid.
41. Ibid., p. 247.

so that only a few will actually experience this horrible suffering. C. S. Lewis and others redefine hell, making it unpleasant, but not the awful terror it has usually been described as. Pinnock, however, will have no part in such an endeavor, which he refers to as "taking the hell out of hell." He rejects such an idea because "it breaks the concentration and prevents people from seeing the need for theological renewal on this point."[42]

4. The next point is also a theological point, namely, the issue of justice. How can God inflict endless and therefore, infinite, punishment, in return for what must necessarily be finite sins? This far exceeds the rule of an eye for an eye, a tooth for a tooth, a life for a life. Worse, there is nothing reclamatory or reformatory about such endless punishment. It is simply retribution and vindictiveness.[43]

5. The fifth point is a metaphysical one. If the wicked continue for ever and ever, there is an eternal dualism of good and evil. If God is "all in all" (1 Cor. 15:28) and makes "all things new" (Rev. 21:5), how can there continue to be, for all eternity, people who are still in rebellion against him?[44]

6. Pinnock realizes that there will be the objection that numerous biblical texts appear to contradict this view he is espousing. What about these? He replies that they are few and can be reconciled with the texts that teach the destruction of the wicked. He replies to certain of these in particular.

- The reference to "their worm does not die and the fire is not quenched" in Mark 9:48 must be understood in light of Isaiah 66:24. It is the worm and the fire that do not die or cease, not the persons.
- "These will go away into eternal punishment" (Matt. 25:46). While it is possible to read the idea of everlasting punishment out of this verse, Pinnock thinks that is not necessary. Jesus does not define the nature of eternal life or eternal death in this passage. He simply says there are two destinies and leaves it at that.
- What about the parable of the rich man and Lazarus? We should recognize, from the reference to Abraham's bosom,

42. Ibid., p. 254.
43. Ibid., p. 255.
44. Ibid., p. 255.

that we are dealing here with imagery, not literal descriptions. Besides that, this is a reference to the intermediate state, not the final condition, and therefore not relevant here.

- What about the references to the lake of fire in Revelation 14? First, we should notice that the reference is actually to the fate of the false prophet, the beast, and certain evildoers. Only in verse 11 are human beings involved, and "it is likely that what is being described is the moment of their judgment, not their everlasting condition, with the smoke going up forever being the testimony to their final destruction."[45]

Pinnock therefore concludes that there is adequate biblical basis for the view of annihilation or destruction of the impenitent. He contends, however, that more than purely exegetical considerations are involved here. People question the traditional position initially, not on biblical grounds but because of its moral implications. He grants that reasoning goes into the process, but notes that the other view relies heavily on tradition. Finally, he observes that a great deal of cultural and situational input goes into the traditional view, including the Hellenistic philosophy mentioned earlier. In light of all these considerations, he believes that the more adequate view is that rather than punishment as torture that continues forever, the wicked are simply destroyed, and that destruction has everlasting effects.[46]

## Evaluation

This movement has garnered considerable attention and provoked a significant amount of discussion in evangelical circles in recent years. As might be expected, it displays both strengths and weaknesses.

### *Positive*

1. These theologians have displayed genuine concern about humans and their fate. Theology at its best is not merely a theoretical matter, a sort of intellectual game,

45. Ibid., pp. 256–57.
46. Ibid., p. 258.

but touches real life, involving the emotions and having definite implications for ministry applications. While at times the pathos becomes excessive, the seriousness of this theology must not be understated.

2. The inclusivists have given needed emphasis to the doctrine of general revelation. Some evangelicals have neglected this doctrine, or have minimized the role and efficacy of general revelation, thinking thereby to preserve a loftier place for special revelation. There is, however, a significant biblical witness to the reality of general revelation, and special revelation is not honored by ignoring this. They have endeavored to give it a rightful place in theology.

3. They have correctly observed that if it is possible to know something of truth about God from general revelation, then this applies to persons from other religions, as well as to philosophers and lay persons. Other religions are not merely totally in error. Their genuine insights need to be recognized. Further, these provide the Christian evangelist with a needed point of contact for carrying on conversations with persons from other religions.

4. These theologians have done a favor to all Christians by calling attention to biblical texts that are sometimes overlooked in discussions of these topics. While those are not always easy to integrate into an existing theology, they make a valuable contribution, as well as providing an important exercise for one's theological method.

5. Postconservatives have frankly faced the fact that factors other than simply Scripture enter into our theological work. The presence of such factors calls not only for recognition, but also for concerted effort to integrate them with the use of Scripture. By so doing, they have moved the debate to the real issues in the differences among evangelicals.

### Negative

1. The desire to see something be the case has apparently led to reading those matters into the biblical text at

some points. For example, while Paul certainly seems to allow for the possibility that people may be saved through general revelation, he does not tell us how many, if any, are saved this way. Indeed, as one continues on through the Book of Romans, Paul appears quite pessimistic about the status of these persons. He seems to be saying, in Romans 10, in effect, "Don't count on their being saved through general revelation. These people need the gospel taken to them."

2. The cases cited as biblical examples of people saved through general revelation are, at best, ambiguous. Certainly, Mechizedek was within the circle of salvation, but how did he get there? We simply do not know enough about him to discern whether that was through the knowledge obtained by general revelation or whether Yahweh may have specially appeared to him, as he did to Abraham. The contention that Cornelius, as a "god-fearer," was already saved prior to his conversation with Peter is contradicted by Peter's statement in Acts 11:14, which forces Sanders to use some very forced exegesis of this passage.

3. The 1 Peter passage advanced in terms of a postmortem encounter is a very difficult one, and its interpretation is widely disputed. It seems strange to hinge such an important doctrine on such equivocal evidence. Further, even if the correct interpretation of the passage is that Jesus descended into Hades and preached the gospel to those who were there, that only takes care of those people. To conclude that the same opportunity is given to sinners who live and die since that time requires an additional step in the argument, a step that unfortunately is never supplied.

4. The annihilation Scriptures are also questionable. The suggestion that the parable of Lazarus and the rich man cannot be used because the central thrust of the passage is otherwise assumes that a passage can teach only one thing—a questionable assumption. That a passage cannot teach contradictory things is one thing; that it cannot teach complementary messages is quite another. Further, the crucial passage, Matthew 25:41,

46, which even John A. T. Robinson admits does not allow distinction between the meaning of eternal life and eternal punishment,[47] is not adequately dealt with.

5. These theologians are quick to disavow universalism, and it would be unfair to identify them with that belief. They continue to refer to Scriptures, however, which are used by universalists to support their position, and to interpret them in similar ways. It is not clear just what safeguards are built into this theology to guarantee that its followers will not draw the inference that universalists have from these passages.

6. The philosophical argument that the theological belief in the immortality of the soul derives from Greek philosophy, specifically that of Plato, is faulty. Not only does this commit the genetic fallacy; it also ignores significant differences between Plato's view and the position under discussion here. Plato believed in the immortality of the soul in both directions, backward and forward. Souls are uncreated and eternal. This is not the case with the Christian doctrine in question.

7. In Pinnock's thought, there seems to be a logical inconsistency between belief in salvation through general revelation and postmortem encounter. Sanders contrasts the two. The problem then surfaces in the dilemma whether those who have the opportunity to believe, following death, are all persons who have not heard during this life, or only those who have made a positive response to that general revelation.

47. John A. T. Robinson, *In the End, God* (New York: Harper and Row, 1968), p. 131, n. 8.

# 6 Where to from Here?

**Having** surveyed the background and development to date of this theological movement, one major question about it remains: What may we expect to see in the years ahead? Prognostication is never easy in any field, particularly in a period of such rapid cultural change as we have recently and are currently seeing. Nonetheless, certain indicators can be observed that will give us some guidance. And being able to anticipate some developments will be the key to our being prepared to make intelligent and effective responses.[1]

In attempting to make such a forecast, it is helpful to summarize some of the general characteristics of this movement:

1. There is a sense of engagement with the spirit of the times, expressed in the idea that theology must be aware of and respond to contemporary cultural movements. In some cases, there is a conscious endeavor to express the theology in light of these forces and movements; in other cases, the influence is more unconscious and tacit.
2. There is an openness to dialogue with those of a more liberal orientation, which exceeds the desire for interaction with those from a more conservative perspective.[2]

1. For a more complete treatment of theological prognostication, the reader is referred to an earlier work by this author, *Where Is Theology Going?* (Grand Rapids: Baker, 1993), especially chapter 1 on the method of theological forecasting.
2. Roger E. Olson, "Whales and Elephants: Both God's Creatures But Can They Meet?" *Pro Ecclesia* 4.2 (Spring 1995): 165–89.

3.  Many of these theologians are reacting against their past, which was in most cases of a more conservative orientation. This is most conspicuous in the case of Clark Pinnock, but also appears in the biographies of other theologians as well. This shift can be documented and is continuing. In some cases, this shift is accompanied by a strongly emotional overtone.

4.  The changes have advanced from one doctrinal area to another. So, for example, the redefining tended to begin with the doctrine of Scripture, especially with biblical inerrancy, which was considered a somewhat peripheral issue. The changes have, however, expanded to other doctrines, such as the nature of God and the extent of salvation.

5.  There is something of a shift from a theocentric to a more anthropocentric orientation in this theology. This has a number of manifestations. It involves, for example, the idea that humanity must be served, and that its perceived needs and temporal welfare should be met by God. There is also, however, an epistemological anthropocentrism, so that humans are the judges of what is true and good. There is considerably more confidence in humans' ability to know and do the good than was true in an earlier evangelicalism.

6.  There is a sense of continuity with the truly orthodox tradition in Christian theology. The more recent evangelicalism, that of the earlier twentieth century, is believed to have distorted the authentic evangelical tradition by its historical and cultural conditioning. These postconservative evangelicals see themselves alternately, and sometimes simultaneously, as giving a more contemporary expression to the evangelical Christian faith and of restoring a more original faith.

7.  These are younger men, for whom the ravages of liberalism on the Christian faith are simply something heard and read about, not experienced firsthand. From their perspective, "establishment evangelicalism" seems overly concerned with preserving truth, by fighting again the battles of an earlier generation.

Where might these theologians be expected to move, in the years ahead? A number of scenarios can be conceived.

## A Further Shift Leftward

Some of these persons will continue moving farther left. Their experience with the strictures of conservative theology drive their theological enterprise more powerfully than does fear of any possible debilitation by liberal thought.

For many of these theologians, however, there is an emotional attachment to certain traditional positions, or at least, to certain traditional practices, which will serve as a deterrent to going too far toward liberalism. Just as Nels Ferré continued to have an hour of personal devotions and an hour of family devotions as he had done as a child, long after his understanding of God and Christ had changed markedly, so we can expect the distance between practice and belief to widen for these people, while they continue to maintain some anchorage in the earlier piety.

*The next generation.* The next generation of postconservatives may be somewhat different, however. They will not have had the experiences associated with the older theology that at least produces a sort of nostalgia for that faith. Thus, they will have even less motivation to preserve the heritage. Consequently, we can expect to see them taking some of the tendencies found in this generation to greater extremes. This may well cause some disappointment and reaction on the part of the generation of theologians we have been examining.

An example from the past can be seen in the death of God theologians, who of course represented a much more radical theology than these men are part of. In a number of cases, they had come from a neoorthodox theological background, in which there was little if any apologetic support of the traditional type, for the theology involved. The certitude of God was found in a direct encounter initiated by God. For some of them, however, there was a sense that the encounter that they had presumably known was not really occurring. And, like the child who declared that the emperor's new clothes were not real, they disavowed any sort of encounter of this type, and with it threw out the idea of any kind of transcendent God at all. Paul

Tillich was disturbed to find that some of the death of God theologians felt they were simply taking his ground of being concept to a more logical conclusion. It is quite possible that we will see a development of this type.

*A cyclical reaction.* At some point, however, a reaction will occur. In our earlier work, we suggested that theology runs in cycles that in some ways resemble economic cycles. In tracing economics back more than four hundred years, it is interesting that economic booms and crashes have historically tended to occur on approximately a sixty-year cycle, such as the financial panic of 1871 and the stock market crash of 1929 and the ensuing depression. One explanation for this is that these declines, sometimes dramatic, occur when a large enough number of consumers and investors arises that have not experienced the preceding hardship. In terms of the twin motivations of greed and fear, they have only really known the former. So excesses occur, in extended indebtedness and overheated stock markets. The mania that follows leads to a sharp overreaction, when things turn in the opposite direction. A purging of the system prepares matters for another advance.[3]

It appears that a parallel situation may be at work in the postconservative evangelical movement. There is a disparagement of the apprehensiveness of older theologians and Christians in general regarding the dangers of eroded theology. This is strangely reminiscent of the impatience of younger consumers and investors, with the caution of those who experienced the last depression and fear the possibility of another one. "It's different this time," is the cry of young investors and mutual fund managers, some of whom, however, in moderate "corrections" exclaim, "I never thought I could lose this much of my portfolio this quickly."

Similarly, these theologians have not seen at close hand the unfortunate effects of liberal theology. Yet at some point, the same decline that has struck the "mainline" (or "sideline") de-

---

3. The thoughtful reader will perhaps observe that we are now overdue for such an economic reversal. The cycle may be getting somewhat longer, due to the increased life expectancy that keeps those who remember the great depression alive longer as a moderating influence in the mix of the economy.

nominations will come close to home. Then, some sort of reaction will take place.

Interestingly, this reaction may come from those already farther left than postconservative evangelicals. The turn of much Protestant theology came, not from a longtime conservative, but from Karl Barth, who had been steeped in liberalism and saw its paucity.[4] So, we are already beginning to see some leftward-moving evangelicals, being passed on the theological roadway by some evangelicals who are coming from more liberal backgrounds and are moving to the right. Thomas Oden and Alister McGrath are notable examples of the latter.

This lack of personal experience of liberalism gives a different quality to this theology than that of postliberalism, even when the formal doctrinal content may be quite similar. I recall in this connection what my doctoral mentor, William Hordern, said on one occasion in class. He was asked about some persons who were moving directly from a conservative theology to neoorthodoxy, without ever having been convinced liberals. He indicated that he and others like him, who like Karl Barth, the founder of the movement, had come to neoorthodoxy out of a more liberal background, felt that such former conservatives lacked something. They needed to have seen the bankruptcy of liberalism firsthand. It may be significant that Karl Barth, throughout his career, continued to move toward a progressively more conservative position. This may not be the case with postconservative evangelicals, however.

*The effect of conversation partners.* Another factor that may well cause postconservatives to continue moving to the left, at least for the time being, is the primary conversation partners of these theologians. As noted earlier, there is a definite openness to the left and a desire to engage in theological dialogue with postliberals in particular. This is accentuated by a reduced discussion with more conservative evangelicals, for whom they reserve and toward whom they direct their strongest criticisms. The dialogue with postliberals is not necessarily for the purpose of convincing these conversation partners to adopt an evangelical or more conservative theology. There is

4. Thomas F. Torrance, *Karl Barth: An Introduction to His Early Theology, 1910–1931* (Naperville, Ill.: Allenson, 1962).

an intention to learn mutually from one another. This should have the effect of continuing the movement toward the left. Thus, for example, postconservatives show a strong preference for narrative theology over propositional theology, but have not tended, in this endeavor, to utilize contemporary narratives or biography, at least not overtly so. If, however, they continue to engage in dialogue with neoliberals while espousing the presuppositions of someone like Terrence Tilley, we may well expect to see such heuristic use of contemporary narratives beginning to appear. Indeed, Grenz's focus on the faith of the community seems naturally disposed toward this. Another indication of this specific move is the appointment of James McClendon to the Fuller Seminary faculty. A decade ago he would not have been considered an evangelical by most evangelicals. His "theology as biography" represents this use of contemporary life stories as a source of theology. Without acknowledging any change in his approach, it has now become a source of theology at an evangelical seminary, in fact, at the flagship postconservative evangelical seminary.

*The effect of presuppositions.* One of the things that we can expect, in this scenario, is the growing influence of the postconservatives' presuppositions on their theology. Here we have some guidance, growing out of the fact that they share some of the presuppositions of more liberal theologians, including some that go back to a generation ago. We can expect two developments, paralleling those of the more liberal thought. One is for a more complete effect of these presuppositions in the areas already discussed, such as the doctrine of God and the doctrine of salvation. The other would be the spread of this influence to other doctrines not yet discussed.

One notable presupposition is the functionalism that appears especially in the doctrine of revelation. This can be expected to reduce the doctrines to those things that can be experienced. Thus, we may expect continued deemphasis on some of the attributes of God. In particular, since we are unable to experience God's infinity directly, those attributes, such as omnipotence and omniscience, may well be diminished. In addition, certain of God's moral attributes do not seem to have great functional value and may well decline. That this is already taking place to some extent can be seen in Pinnock's repeated strong objections to Augustine's doctrination of predestination, which especially appears to conflict with human need and human welfare at a number of points. We may expect deemphasis of the moral attributes of holiness, wrath, judgment, and the like. Indeed, lessened certainty about the essential attributes of God that do not enter practical experience is likely. Note, for example, the rather constricted treatment of the attributes already present in the work of these theologians. To be sure, their writing to date has been primarily motivated by objection to the disputed aspects of the classical view. Thus, the attributes of omnipresence, omnipotence, simplicity, and goodness, for example, really are not discussed. It may be that these will come in for later consideration, or it may also be that they will simply not get any treatment at the hands of these theologians, and that there will be something of a lacuna in their thought.

There are other areas where we may expect this functional-existential conception of truth to exert influence. One of these is Christology. In broader theological circles, functional Christology became quite popular a generation or so ago, through the influence of theologians and biblical scholars such as Oscar Cullmann. The basic thrust of this Christology is that the New Testament writers were not concerned with metaphysical questions, with questions of the nature of Jesus. They did not ask about what Jesus was, or even, in a sense, who he was. Rather, they discussed what he did. The person of Christ was approached through the work of Christ. Thus, speculation about two natures and one person was considered philosophical rather than biblical. In some versions of functional Christology, the Chalcedonian formulation was considered a legitimate inference from the biblical materials. In others, however, it was considered an intrusion of extraneous philosophical influences. There has been relative silence, at least in print, on Christology by postconservatives. Roger Olson, drawing primarily on his knowledge of the evangelical theology section of the American Academy of Religion, suggests that there is a stronger emphasis on the humanity versus the primary deity of Jesus Christ. In his judgment, postconservatives are more likely to think of the deity of Christ relationally, in terms of his special relationship of unity with the Father.[5] It seems likely that future de-

5. Roger E. Olson, "Postconservative Evangelicals Greet the Postmodern Age," *Christian Century* 112.15 (May 3, 1995): 482.

velopments here will be in this direction, particularly in terms of the functional approach to Christology.

Ironically, this tendency to draw on presuppositions in theology from thirty to fifty years ago puts postconservatives in a rather awkward situation. For the functional Christology of Cullmann and others was based on a particular conception of the relationship of Greek and Hebrew thinking. The familiar position of the biblical theology movement was that the true biblical thought was Hebraic—very concrete, nontheoretical, nonspeculative, unconcerned about metaphysical-type questions. The Greek mind, on the other hand, was much more metaphysical. In some cases, the influence of Greek thinking was believed to have come in after the biblical period, but some of the "biblical theology" thinkers regarded it as already having entered the New Testament, and thus having perverted purer biblical tradition.

One can see this type of presupposition at work in a number of places in the postconservative evangelicals' theology, especially in their criticisms of the older tradition. It appears, for example, in the criticism of the classical view of God, in which Greek philosophy is believed to have perverted the true biblical view within the history of the church. It can also be found in Pinnock's criticism of the idea of the immortality of the soul, in connection with his advocacy of annihilation.

The ironic thing about this particular presupposition of the theology we are studying is that it has come under heavy criticism in broader theological circles, beginning as long ago as the early 1960s. The most effective salvo was fired by James Barr, especially in his *Semantics of Biblical Language*.[6] Barr, at one time himself an evangelical, has for some time been no supporter of evangelical theology, as witnessed by his *Fundamentalism*.[7] Yet his criticism of the biblical theology movement's view of the Hebrew and Greek mind is devastating in its effect. He contends that the theory about the respective natures of the two mentalities simply does not fit the characteristics of the languages themselves. By the use of linguistics he shows

6. James Barr, *The Semantics of Biblical Language* (London: Oxford University Press, 1961).

7. James Barr, *Fundamentalism* (Philadelphia: Westminster, 1977).

the artificiality of the assumptions on which much of that theology rested. Indeed, Brevard Childs wrote of the "crumbling of the walls," of the biblical theology movement, one of which was the "distinctive biblical mentality." He said of Barr's book, "Seldom has one book brought down so much theological superstructure with such effectiveness."[8]

In my early days of seminary teaching in the 1970s, I frequently found students who repeated in my classes the teaching they were receiving from two New Testament professors at that school about functional Christology and the influence of Greek thought. When questioned about the writings of Barr, Childs, and others, they gave me blank looks. Their unawareness of those challenges to the biblical theology synthesis reflected a serious gap in their scholarly preparation. It is almost incredible, however, to hear the same clichés being repeated a quarter of a century later. The point being made here does not require that one accept Barr's conclusions, although they are rather widely acknowledged. It does, however, require some response. To continue to repeat the old contentions without taking some account of this type of scholarship will doom these postconservatives to eventual irrelevance with some of their more liberal potential dialogue partners. Eventually, of course, this neglect will catch up with postconservatives and force some sort of adjustment in their view.

Another area where we may see the effect of functionalist presuppositions is in the doctrine of salvation. Thus far, the major attention with respect to this doctrine has been given to the question of the extent of salvation, or who will be saved, and the means by which that salvation is mediated to the person. There has not been a great deal of discussion about the nature of salvation. The one exception to this seems to be Pinnock's contention that salvation includes healing, or at least that it did in Peter's statement in Acts 4:12. However, as the effects of these presuppositions progress, we may well find less interest in the traditional loci of regeneration, justification, and so on. There may well be a greater emphasis on the temporal dimensions of salvation, even involving more of a social gospel.

8. Brevard Childs, *Biblical Theology in Crisis* (Philadelphia: Westminster, 1970), p. 72.

Since virtually all definitions of evangelicalism ordinarily include the idea of salvation by grace, in particular, the emphasis on individual regeneration, this, if it occurs, will strain the evangelical orientation of the postconservative theology.

*External influences.* While we have noted the influence of some earlier factors, we also must take into account the growing influence of present external ones. As we have noted, these theologians are very sensitive to the contemporary secular environment, and want to formulate their theology in such a way as to make an adequate response to it. This is especially the case with postmodernism, most notably with Grenz's reaction to it. Although we have not gone into this response in any depth, we should note the somewhat ambiguous nature of that response. Grenz is quite clear that the modern period either has given way to the postmodern, or is definitely doing so. Yet, he says, of some of the more extreme tendencies within postmodernism, as evangelicals we cannot go all the way with postmodernism.[9] He does not really give any basis for not accepting the full implications of these premises, however. At some point, this reticence will have to be faced and either justified or abandoned. At that point, the theology will either become more radical and more subjective, or less so. Which direction he moves in that situation will be very interesting to observe.

Both Grenz and Thomas Oden consider themselves postmodern. Actually, Oden does not refer to what often is labeled postmodernism by that title, but rather calls it "ultramodern," taking to extremes tendencies already at work within the modern period. Yet their reactions are quite different. Oden is moving away from the relativizing influences, drawing more heavily on earlier classic Christianity. Whether such a reversal of direction will also be found in Grenz's case remains to be seen.

It is quite possible that we will see the spread of this postconservative reconstruction into other doctrines as well. It remains to be seen what will happen to the doctrine of sin, but it is notable that there is really relatively little discussion of it. Based

---

9. Stanley J. Grenz, "Star Trek and the Next Generation: Postmodernism and the Future of Evangelical Theology," in *The Challenge of Postmodernism: An Evangelical Engagement*, ed. David S. Dockery (Wheaton, Ill.: Victor, 1995), pp. 99, 101.

on the assumptions at work here, it seems unlikely that the traditional form of the doctrine of sin will be prominent in the future. This would seem to follow from the anthropocentric dimensions of this theology. The same may or may not be true of the doctrine of Satan. One would expect that this would be muted, in keeping with the anthropocentrism just mentioned. Yet the very opposite might be the case. Pinnock, for example, has shown a strong interest in the charismatic variety of Christianity, and this frequently includes an extensive belief in the spirit world. In addition, as greater attention is given to the problem of evil, the fixation of responsibility on humans may not be permanent. This theology at times appears to be more an anthropodicy, or justification of humanity, than a theodicy, or justification of God. If this is the case, then a firm belief in the reality and activity of Satan could be expected.

One reason why such a spread may well take place is that, as I have often written, theology is organic. Thus, to the extent that logical implications are thoroughly worked out, the conclusion drawn in one area will affect conclusions in other areas as well. We can see this in two instances in Clark Pinnock's theology, where the doctrine of God and the doctrine of salvation are tied together. Regardless of which preceded which, the spillover effect is noticeable.

One of these pertains to God's foreknowledge. Pinnock, as we have seen, postulates that God would not send anyone to hell without giving each person a chance to accept the gift of salvation, or at least, without knowing how that person would have responded if given such an opportunity. Since God does not and cannot know contingent future human decisions and actions, however, he must give each person that opportunity, or God would never know whether the person would have believed. This requires a postmortem encounter.

The other area relates to impassibility. Pinnock and his fellow free will theists believe that God feels our hurts and suffers with suffering humanity. If this is the case, however, then if there is a hell of eternal suffering, God would presumably be miserable throughout eternity, suffering with these finally impenitent. The doctrine of annihilation is therefore necessary to prevent God's unending misery.

## A Reversal toward Conservatism

*Work of Christian philosophers.* There is, however, the possibility of a move back toward a more conservative position. This might come about through a number of influences. One of these is the work of some conservative Christian philosophers. Two who come particularly to mind are Alvin Plantinga and Thomas Morris, both members of the department of philosophy at the University of Notre Dame. While not necessarily following all the details of Calvinism, they do come out at basically more traditional positions than do the free will theists on such attributes as the foreknowledge and even the immutability of God. Because the issues under dispute in this discussion are largely philosophical, it may well be that such influential philosophers will influence the free will theists to accept the viability of a more traditional view of God.

*Third world Christianity.* The other major influence that will begin increasingly to come to bear on these theologians is the growth of third world theology. It is in places like Latin America, Africa, and Asia that the church is expanding most rapidly. By the year 2000, for example, it is estimated that there will be 400 million Christians in Africa. Not only are Christians more numerous in these areas, and becoming ever more so, but there is also a greater vitality, a stronger sense of commitment, in this branch of the Christian church. Thus far, the third world has produced relatively little theology. As the church matures, however, coming to the stage where it is able to give attention to such matters as theology, we can expect to see a rapid increase in the flow of this scholarly production. Since postconservatives have declared their intention to include theologians of different races and cultures and both genders in theological discussion, we can expect that they will experience some influence from these third world Christian theologians.

What will be the nature of this influence? Will it be a factor moving theology to the left or to the right? In some ways, these third world persons will probably have quite a lot of affinity with some of the ideas of postconservatives. For example, they tend not to be as rationalistic as Westerners, insisting on the logical consistency of all that is held. They will probably give greater place to factors such as intuition.

On the other hand, however, there will be some major differences in terms of the more conservative orientation of third world Christians and presumably also theologians. This will show itself in a number of ways. One is a strong sense of the supernatural. Not only is there a greater openness to the supernatural and a lesser naturalistic bias, but there actually appears to be more experience of the supernatural. In third world countries, it seems as if God is actually performing more miracles than in some more established areas of the church's presence. There also is a stronger sense of the antithesis between God and good on the one hand, and evil and sin on the other. In some of these countries, evil takes very vivid and very powerful form. In Africa, for example, where witch doctors are still prevalent and Satan worship is to be found, and in countries where colonial exploitation is still well remembered, where there has been totalitarian government until recently, or where social and racial injustices still linger, evil is definitely believed in. The difference between Christianity and the world or other religions is quite evident to Christians in less developed countries.

These characteristics will tend to produce effects in two major doctrinal areas. One is the doctrine of God. The idea of a limited God will not appeal to these Christians. They will have a strong belief in an all-powerful, all-knowing, good God. Further, their religion will not be as anthropocentric as that of postconservatives. They will be more inclined to submit in obedience to an all-powerful, sovereign God than to seek to make that God satisfy their needs and their beliefs.

There will probably also be a strongly exclusivistic approach to the doctrine of salvation. Given the background of Christianity's difference from the alternatives and the cost that some third world Christians have had to pay to be Christians, it seems unlikely that a very inclusivistic understanding of the gospel will be very appealing to them. There will be a skepticism about some of what will appear to them to be rather romantic ideas about the extent and influence of common grace in the human race and society generally.

There will also be a more conservative view of the Bible. Rather than complex methods of criticism and interpretation, these Christians will show a much greater tendency to take bib-

lical statements at face value. And with a lesser concern for mi-
nutia of the biblical text, some of the problem passages appealed to in opposition to the idea of biblical inerrancy will not
carry much weight.

It also seems unlikely that the sense of need for updating or
revisioning theology will be very strong with these Christians.
Postmodernism in the intellectual form being discussed by
postconservatives has not really reached the societies of many
of these people. Indeed, in some cases, they are scarcely into
the modern period in certain respects.

There should be some significant impact of such third world
theology on postconservatives, because they have expressed
strong desire to make theology more diverse, more inclusive of
minority and global viewpoints. Thus, whereas postconservatives are not now really doing much dialoguing with persons
more conservative than them, and are concentrating more on
conversations with liberals, this should be a more conservative
group with which they would seek and encourage discussion.

In practice, there is no real evidence that this is being done
thus far. Grenz, for example, although urging a revisioned
theology responsive to postmodernism, has not really carried
through certain facets of that in his *Theology for the Community of God*. A perusal of the index indicates a strong preoccu-
pation with European and North American theologians.
There are sixteen index references to Barth, sixteen to Calvin,
seven to Hegel, six to Kant, eighteen to Luther, nineteen to
Pannenberg, ten to Schleiermacher, fourteen to Thomas
Aquinas, even sixteen to Erickson, only one each to Daly,
Cone, McFague, Ruether, and Soelle, and none to Gutierrez,
Sobrino, Boff, Pobee, Kachura, Kitamori, or any other third
world voices. This is traditional, Western, male, white, Euro-
centric middle-class theology. The same is true of the other
postconservatives, the one real exception being William Dyrness.[10] Hopefully, this will change, and when that happens, if

10. William A. Dyrness, *Christian Apologetics in a World Community*
(Downers Grove, Ill.: InterVarsity, 1983); *Learning about Theology from the
Third World* (Grand Rapids: Zondervan, 1990); *Invitation to Cross-Cultural
Theology: Case Studies in Vernacular Theologies* (Grand Rapids: Zondervan,
1992); *Emerging Voices in Global Christian Theology* (Grand Rapids: Zonder-
van, 1994).

there is genuine openness to the ideas of the third world thinkers, as more evangelical theologians begin speaking and writing, some postconservatives may well shift back toward a more conservative position.

## Reactions to Postconservative Evangelical Theology

The nature of reactions to this postconservative evangelical theology will be interesting to observe. Thus far, there has been dialogue with postliberals, but not a great deal of reaction or evaluation by that group. What there is has tended to be positive, but it remains to be seen whether postliberals will see postconservatives as being of a common mind with them, or only thinly veneered versions of the old conservatism, or whether they will be skeptical of postconservatives for reasons such as William Hordern gave regarding conservatives moving directly into neoorthodoxy.

There have been different reactions on the part of more traditional evangelicals. Some of these have been careful, measured, scholarly assessments and critiques. The reviews of *The Openness of God* by Alister McGrath and Timothy George seem to fall into this category.[11] In general, most evangelicals on the right have been moving more toward the center, becoming more tempered and willing to discuss theology with those less conservative. Fundamentalism of the type of the 1920s and 1930s is less prevalent, although, of course, some evangelicals will continue to move farther to the right.

## Evangelical or Not?

A final question concerns whether this movement should continue to be considered evangelical. Here, interestingly, we may note that really the only charge that one's opponent is not evangelical is that leveled by Pinnock against those who differ from him on the possibility of persons who have not heard of Christ being saved. He says, "What does 'evangelical' mean

11. Alister E. McGrath, "Whatever Happened to Luther?" *Christianity Today* 39.1 (January 9, 1995): 34; Timothy George, "A Transcendence-Starved Deity," *Christianity Today* 39.1 (January 9, 1995): 33–34.

when applied to those who seem to want to ensure that there is as little Good News as possible?"[12]

Some evangelicals are raising the question, however, of whether this view is really consistently evangelical, or whether it is actually partway between the evangelical view and some nonevangelical position on certain issues. Thus, for example, these men have acknowledged that their view stands midway between the classical view of God and that of process theology.[13] Similarly, a number of persons have suggested that Grenz's view of revelation has considerable affinity for the neoorthodox view,[14] or that it actually stands midway between the neoorthodox and the orthodox or evangelical view.[15] Donald Carson is more unequivocal: "With the best will in the world, I cannot see how Grenz's approach to Scripture can be called 'evangelical' in any useful sense."[16]

The question, however, becomes one of how far one may move, or how many times one may halve the distance between things, and still claim to be within the original group. Here we encounter what I would term a theological version of Zeno's paradox, but in reverse. Zeno was a Greek philosopher who contended that motion and change were illusory. He did this by the use of a paradox. To move from A to B, he said, one must first move from A to C, which is halfway to B. But before one can do

12. Clark Pinnock, *A Wideness in God's Mercy* (Grand Rapids: Zondervan, 1992), p. 163.

13. Richard Rice, *God's Foreknowledge and Man's Free Will* (Minneapolis: Bethany, 1985), p. 33; Clark H. Pinnock, "Between Classical and Process Theism," in *Process Theology*, ed. Ronald Nash (Grand Rapids: Baker, 1987), pp. 313–14.

14. R. Albert Mohler Jr., "The Integrity of the Evangelical Tradition and the Challenge of the Postmodern Paradigm," in *The Challenge of Postmodernism*, pp. 78–81; Glenn Galloway, *The Efficacy of Propositionalism: The Challenge of Philosophical Linguistics and Literary Theory to Evangelical Theology*, unpublished Ph.D. dissertation, Southern Baptist Theological Seminary, 1966, pp. 207–11.

15. Norman Gulley, *Systematic Theology*, unpublished manuscript, vol. 1, *Prolegomena*, pp. 269–73. Cf. Henry A. Knight, III, "True Affections: Biblical Narrative and Evangelical Spirituality," in *The Nature of Confession: Evangelicals and Postliberals in Conversation*, ed. Timothy R. Phillips and Dennis L. Okholm (Downers Grove, Ill.: InterVarsity, 1996), pp. 197–98.

16. D. A. Carson, *The Gagging of God* (Grand Rapids: Zondervan, 1996), p. 481.

that, he must move from A to D, which is halfway from A to C. Before doing that, however, one must move from A to E, which is halfway from A to D. Thus, one can never get there. Now the issue here is this. Suppose we determine the outside edges of evangelicalism (A) and neoorthodoxy (B), for example. Then suppose we have a view which is halfway from A to B. Or perhaps it is only 40 percent of the way from A to B, so that it is closer to evangelicalism than to neoorthodoxy. Is this point then considered to be evangelicalism? Seemingly it should be that, since it is closer to that than it is neoorthodoxy. But suppose, further, that this theologian subsequently moves 40 percent of the way from C to B? Is this new position, closer to what was now called evangelicalism, to be considered evangelical, even though it is closer to neoorthodoxy than to the original limit of evangelicalism? Although on this model it will never get all the way to neoorthodoxy, when is it no longer entitled to be called evangelical? If a waterfowl looks like a duck and quacks like a duck, but walks like a goose, is it still a duck? If it then honks like a goose and walks like a goose but still looks like a duck, is it a duck or a goose? Surely there must come some point where the line has been crossed, and at least a hybrid must be present. It does not yet appear that these theologians have moved so far as to surrender the right to be called evangelicals, but such movement cannot be unlimited.

# Scripture Index

# Subject Index

Millard J. Erickson is Distinguished Professor of Theology at Baylor University's Truett Seminary and at Western Seminary, Portland. He is a leading evangelical spokesman with numerous volumes to his credit, including *Christian Theology, Introducing Christian Doctrine, God in Three Persons, The Word Became Flesh, The Evangelical Heart and Mind,* and *Where Is Theology Going?*